DEPARDIEU

DEPARDIEU

MARIANNE GRAY

SINCLAIR-STEVENSON

First published in Great Britain by
Sinclair-Stevenson Limited
7/8 Kendrick Mews
London SW7 3HG England

British Library Cataloguing in Publication Data
A CIP catalogue record for this book is available from the British Library.

ISBN: 1 85619 0 951

Typeset by Butler & Tanner Ltd,
Printed and bound in Great Britain by
Butler & Tanner Ltd, Frome and London.

For Michael
who had to live with a strange man in the house for so long

Contents

Prologue

Gérard Depardieu (pronounced 'deh-par-dyeuh') is a man whose mis-pronounced name is synonymous with controversy. His public image is the most confusing in showbiz and his body of work is as turbulent.

For many he is one of the finest and most prolific actors to emerge from Europe and conquer the rest of the world as a mercurial leading man. For others he is a tough primal hulk with a broken nose, a chin like a shovel, and irresistible animal magnetism. Either way he's destroyed forever the hackneyed image of the conventional male film star, leaving him whimpering in the dust, as he strides around with his ugly good looks, a guy in a hurry in a career that doesn't know how to stop.

The story of his life has been quoted flamboyantly, reworked dozens of times, even used as inspiration for films. Sifting through the details while researching this biography, I came across several versions, some based loosely on fact, concreted into popular mythology. Whether this is by accident or by design barely matters. In the old days the Hollywood studio publicity hacks would have created the hyperbole for him but done only half as good a job.

Either way it is the story of a man with an extraordinary energy and appetite for life on the one hand, an all-round *bon viveur* who embarks on mighty nocturnal benders and emerges grinning wickedly, on the other of a man who is deeply unsure of himself. There is nothing fake about Depardieu. He's tangibly real. You want to make friends with him, take a glass of wine together. He will always be as French as garlic, and as an

1

actor always grip a role by the neck and shake it until it's his.

There's no cause for a slash-and-burn bio with Depardieu. There has been no muck to rake, no scandals in high places, only idiosyncratic anecdotes, quirks and contradictions caused by nobody ever taking the actor aside and telling him to watch his lucid words and ample gestures when confronting the world press – especially when he does so in his heavily accented, approximate English which somebody once described as one-third BBC, two-thirds jukebox.

Then, of course, there has been his impetuous choice of roles, from cold-hearted killers, to a father who castrates himself with an electric carving knife (*La Dernière Femme*) and a hunchback (*Jean de Florette*).

However, he remains the only French actor movie audiences will turn out for in their droves. He has never been the new Montand, Belmondo or Delon. He has always just been Depardieu, no elegant boudoir charmer, injecting his driven energy into films and theatrical pieces. France might have had its Nouvelle Vague (New Wave) in the late 1950s but in the 80s they had Depardieu, a one-man new-wave all of his own, an actor who has set an indelible stamp on his country's films.

No actor of his generation can match his range of roles or have over-stepped the mark quite so far. None has worked with such manic effort and rogue spirit to get there to claim the acting crown. And like Maurice Chevalier, Charles Boyer and Louis Jourdan, he has also made it across the Atlantic. In 1990 he was given the Golden Globe for best comedy actor in *Green Card*.

At the time of going to press he will have made seventy films since he started in 1971, some utterly beguiling, like *Jean de Florette* and *Martin Guerre*, others frankly awful, like the disastrous *One Woman or Two* made with Sigourney Weaver and a female fossil. He has also done an assortment of stagework and, in his early days, some French television. Various awards highlight this career on an international scale. His book of poignant thoughts on his life and the people who inhabited it, *Lettres Volées (Stolen Letters)*, is, for a celebrity, a revelation and the albums of songs written for him by his wife of more than twenty years, Elisabeth, a sheer delight.

However, just when the English-speaking world was courting him as their new discovery – the thinking woman's bit of muscle, the discerning man's hero – the swashbuckling actor was swept from his pinnacle by 'L'Affaire Gérard Depardieu', a ruckus that stemmed from a story in *Time* magazine based on a quotation from an interview given thirteen years earlier to an obscure American film magazine called *Film Comment*. It concerned his early childhood when he claimed to have been involved in a rape (the involvement hung on the translation concerning the French verb *assister*, which means 'to be present at' but appears to have been translated as 'participated in'.)

The Americans were outraged. Nominated for a Best Actor Oscar with British bookies pitting him at 9–2 (against Kevin Costner's 5–2), he was quickly struck off the list; his films, the vastly popular *Green Card* and *Cyrano de Bergerac*, the most successful subtitled film ever, were boycotted.

Hunting Depardieu down and hurling unrelenting criticism at him became something of a cottage industry for press and public alike. His erratic Frenchness took a thorough beating, his bemused trust in people was trampled underfoot and his uncontrived masculinity was spat on. He had been caught by the very thing he had anticipated some years ago when he said, 'Popularity is nice but it's a trap; you have to be on your guard all the time.'

Time magazine refused to retract the passage and Depardieu quietly retired to the Indian Ocean island of Mauritius to make a new film. Suddenly this biography, which started life as a book about an unusual and outstanding actor whose off-screen joy in life is to cultivate fine wines at his château in the Loire Valley, became a controversial document about a man they were calling a rapist.

It is said that when French mountain bears see a particularly imposing member of their species, they exclaim: '*Ah, mon Dieu! Un Depardieu!*' I go along with the bears.

1

Châteauroux

For Gérard Depardieu, it was a liberating childhood experience, growing up with the bravado rock'n'roll values of the American armed forces abroad. Born in a remote small town in Central France with a US Air Force base stapled to its edge, the GI distraction, with its friendly 'hey buddy' ways, not only staved off his fear of being alone, but soon taught him how to hang out like James Dean or Marlon Brando down at the station bar, kicking Coke cans and smoking Camels down to the butt – in short, behaving like *un voyou*.

This word '*voyou*' is still one of Depardieu's favourites. The direct translation is 'hoodlum' or 'hooligan', but the essence is diluted in interpretation, for much of his show of toughness was, and still is, bark rather than bite. Châteauroux friends remember him as a regular guy who liked to see himself as a bit of a warrior, a bit of a wise boy, hawking black-market goods around the American base. One of his major coups was to flog the Americans TV sets, black-and-white ones with a red label stuck to them which said 'Colour'.

But then all the kids got jobs at the base, and if they could get their hands on cheap cigarettes and drink, they sold them for a profit. While for some it was irresistible because it was worldly, for others it was essential because it brought them quick money. For Depardieu it was both.

At the time he was about ten or twelve, an overgrown schoolboy with a quick mind and strong sense of survival on the streets of his dreams. The Châteauroux kid was forged loosely in the Hollywood mould with his

5

attractively open face with wide forehead, heavy chin and a nose he would never quite grow into.

'After the war, with the Americans there, Châteauroux was fantasia for us country boys,' recalls Depardieu. 'It was a true Western movie when the GIs invaded the town with their music, their convertible Buicks, their banana splits and Hawaiian shirts. We had striptease, bars, street-fighting and whores! The Berry was wilder than Cannes or Juan-les-Pins.'

It was this theme of the smalltown *voyou* that he chose to use as his identity from early on. He did it so well that, later, some of his films were to take inspiration from an apparently rowdy boyhood which, according to childhood friend, actor Michel Pilorgé, is sometimes elaborated.

'He loved the mythology,' says Pilorgé, who has since acted with Depardieu, and is clearly amused by the folklore about Depardieu's misspent youth that at times reaches legendary proportions and has bought a dash of headiness to a place that otherwise probably wouldn't have made it beyond the local papers.

Even when the summer skies roll lazily over Châteauroux, Indre-en-Berry, one couldn't call it a charming town. Now billed as 'a town in a garden' since the new Cordeliers Park was opened – by Depardieu in 1980 – it is in fact nondescript and provincial, coloured with grey slate roofs, beige pebble-dashed walls and tightly pollarded plane trees. The River Indre tips the northern edge and a hundred yards from the centre of town is the twenty-square-mile forest of Châteauroux. It is in one of the oldest agricultural regions in the country with flat fields, Charolais cattle and forest-fringed farmland.

There isn't much to do in Châteauroux now that the GIs have gone. Since de Gaulle's modernisation heyday all signs of the American occupation have been wiped away. The town has been restored into bourgeois neatness and the Hôtel de la Gare, where Depardieu remembers passing out in an alcoholic stupor in the *pissoir* aged thirteen, is now painted pink with bright *brasserie* parasols outside. The revamped station is full of gentlemen with briefcases and ladies travelling to see their sisters in Bourges. The kids who used to argue, smoke and spit had, according to my taxi driver, all gone off and got jobs. Yes, Gérard Depardieu was one of them but was no worse than anybody else.

'He wasn't in my gang,' he added, 'but we all did *le business* with the Americans. We had to. France was not a rich place after the war.'

Apart from the hotel, Le Manhattan, in the Place de la Gare, where you can still get a room for sixty francs (about £6), and Le Fésant, where the

6

kids still play the same pinball machines, Châteauroux, capital of the southern Berry, has become the epitome of French middle-class correctness. It passes as a peaceful, undistinguished dot on the map, somewhere between Bourges and Limousin, where motorists stop for petrol between Paris, 263 kilometres almost due north, and the South-West. The only evidence that Gérard Depardieu was born there is the window in the video shop plastered with posters of *Cyrano de Bergerac* with 'Notre Gérard' lovingly lipsticked over it on the outside.

Does the lady behind the counter with glasses and flecked hair remember Monsieur Depardieu? Oh yes, she says, but she finds him too tough for her. Her daughter gives her a withering look and tells her she knows nothing. Hadn't she read the magazine that reported that the American housewife of today regards the archetypal Frenchman as Gérard Depardieu? Her mother mutters that she finds him too brazen. Genteel ladies of a certain generation prefer Chevalier, Aznavour or Delon. But no doubt Châteauroux will soon put a memorial up to their most famous son. Perhaps they should rename the Apollo Cinema after him, for his movies go down well in Châteauroux. They might even put a blue plaque up on his family home.

A modest two-storey bungalow built by his father in 1954, it is in the better part of the wrong side of town. The mayor responsible for building the estate lived round the corner and all kinds of nice people, like retired journalist Maurice Croze, still live there. *Chez* Depardieu is a neat family house with a little garden and fruit trees in the front and a 'Beware of the Dog' sign on the gate. The street it's on is named after Ferdinand de Lesseps, the nineteenth-century engineer who supervised the construction of the Suez Canal. Depardieu's sister Catherine and her husband live there now. Brother Eric lives a few streets away.

Depardieu, however, remembers it as a *cabane* (shack) and a *grotte* (cave), a dark and emotion-choked place where love didn't exist, feelings couldn't grow, conversation was unknown and books weren't read. So many of that generation of peasant-turned-townsfolk hadn't mastered reading and writing, and were too old to learn it in midlife.

His father, René, who signed his name 'D.D.' instead of Depardieu and was called 'Le Dédé', had come in the rural exodus from the backwashes of Berry country where the peasants are bred like those in Brueghel landscapes, bullnecked, with legs like trees, hands like hams and amiable faces. René's father had died in the First World War, leaving only some notebooks calculating the full moon and sunrise. His mother Denise had

Chez Depardieu, rue Ferdinand de Lesseps, Châteauroux

been a medium. Gérard recalls seeing her laying hands on somebody, healing them and coming away pale and wasted. Dédé remembered his childhood full of Berrichon tradition – now only seen re-enacted at folklore festivals – such as wedding celebrations, when the men turned out in big black hats and white stockings, and the women in white mobcaps and long frocks worn with a bank-holiday look, while everyone paraded behind the couple led by somebody playing a bagpipe.

'The Berrichons are strange people,' says Depardieu, proud to be one and always eager to reclaim his peasant heritage. 'They might be hard and closed but when they let themselves break out, there's no limit. It's the cry of the beast. When a Berrichon takes off, he goes a long way!'

When the small-holding peasant life became harder as industrialisation encroached and the search for work set in, René Depardieu left the land at fifteen to become a cobbler, then to do a *tour de France* trade apprenticeship in various towns as a sheet-metal welder. The *pièce de résistance* of his apprenticeship, an articulated wire-mesh boot that can be worn, now stands on show in his son's elegant house outside Paris. Depardieu Senior never happily adapted to urban life and retained deep-seated rural Berry traditions, which, converted to his new lifestyle, meant he refused to weld at full moon.

Eventually he found work in Châteauroux where he was considered an immigrant. Clearly a man who escaped life's problems by drinking and dreaming, he preferred tending his vegetables on his plot of land and fishing to work, and bars to home. His son recounts how he would don his sailor's cap, leap onto his *vélo* and head for the River Indre where industrial waste had killed off the fish and spend the day dreaming of the ocean he never got to see.

Dédé imposed nothing on his son and taught him little. He refused to sign the papers brought to him authorising his son to be sent to reform school after a clash with the police and embarrassed the boy by swaying around drunk outside the school gates. The only time he seemed to involve himself actively in his son's upbringing was to teach him how to hold a fishing rod properly. He clearly caused Gérard heartfelt hardship by rearing such a large family that was destined frequently to live off loans and child allowance.

Depardieu writes angrily in *Lettres Volées* of the shame he felt when his father was drunk. Yet he seems to have clung to what link existed between father and son, and when he formed his own film-production company he called it 'D.D. Productions'.

Depardieu's mother, Eliette, a simple lady with a generous sweep of a nose, was known as La Lilette. She was also a Berrichonne with roots that could never really adapt to town life. Her mother had practised magic, 'black magic' Depardieu revels in calling it, but no magic seemed to have worked for her. Lilette always wanted to be free, to travel, but instead she had six children. Gérard was, he says, the one that sealed her fate and tied her down. He describes her as constantly pregnant, babies popping out of her stomach 'at an industrial rate, like real little ping-pong balls'. He says she gave him what she could, discreetly, to the point of exhaustion but it was never real love.

The house where Gérard Xavier Depardieu (the name an old Berrichon one meaning literally 'Oh my God!') was born on 27 December 1948, the third of six children, was the first Châteauroux home of René and Eliette, a rented place around the corner in rue Pierre et Marie Curie.

That year the first French atomic reactor began to operate at Fort de

At Lycée Jean Giraudoux, directly in front of teacher's desk

Châtillon; Gérard arrived the week Prince Charles was christened and when the sloppy song 'It's Magic' topped the hit parade. For the Depardieu family it was far from magic. Gérard was another mouth to feed, another noisy creature to disturb the repressed silence. Alain and Hélène had already done that. Catherine, Eric and Franck were to do it after Gérard. He comments how he must have been a horrible Christmas present, like the traditional one of the poor, 'an old shoe with an orange in it'.

Although Depardieu romanticises a great deal about his childhood, saying how they were 'poorer than poor', that is not instantly evident when you visit their neatly bourgeois patch. But how one views one's own life is a personal matter. He has said it is good for an actor to be raised in poverty, as 'the poor dream more'; but whatever the truth, his childhood left a lasting mark on him.

10

Obviously a boy with great and unacknowledged sensitivity, Depardieu seems to have grown up deeply affected by the bitterness and hopelessness of his parents. He never had the joy of the family eating together at the same table and recalls awful nights waking up in a sweat plagued by the recurring nightmare of a rat at his jugular vein or dying quietly in his own blood without disturbing the family. He had particular fears of being alone in silence and of being 'snatched by nature'.

'More than anything I was motivated by the fear of boredom, and since that tended to result in confrontation, people came to regard me as a bit of a hooligan. But I was just somebody who needed to get away, to travel. I needed new horizons. If that makes you a hooligan, well, fair enough.' In another family, with his driven imagination and desperate need to avoid being bored in an environment where activity died before it had a chance to be nurtured, he would have been a child with special needs.

Depardieu talks about spending a summer as a child of twelve, living and working for a local farming family at the seaside at Arcachon, just west of Bordeaux, and how he felt family love for the first time in his life. He would return to them when he felt the need for warmth, just for three or four days, for a top-up before going back to Châteauroux to create his own little world once again. He eventually returned there to work for a while as a boatboy on a small passenger vessel in the Bay of Biscay. He was the first member of his family to see the sea.

His mother found him not a bad child but a tough one to keep tabs on.

'We never knew where he'd gone; often the police would bring him back to the house,' she laughingly told Daniel Bernardet, former mayor of Châteauroux, when Gérard returned as the prodigal son, in 1980, to receive the keys of the town.

By the time he was seven or eight he remembers being very tall for his age and no longer considered a child. Some of his friends' parents would not allow him to play with their children because they thought he was a bad influence on them. At twelve he weighed seventy-five kilos and was 1.82 metres tall, and teased for being unnaturally brawny. It is hard to think of him as a stripling. But it was far harder for him to be encumbered by such a provocative packet of flesh.

Although he claims to have carried a gun (a .635) at school and to have been the dunce in his class at the Lycée Jean Giraudoux, records show that at thirteen and a half he actually got his *Certificat d'Etudes*, the diploma one sits at the end of primary school before going on to secondary education. He got it, he adds, without cheating, but all that somehow

11

confuses his claim about being an illiterate urchin who made up for his academic shortcomings with sport. Unhoned maybe and sporting yes, but never stupid or dumb in the basic skills.

His old headmaster, Roger Lucas, remembers that young Depardieu, known as '*deux par deux*' (or even '*trois par trois*'), was a chivalrous kid who defended the smaller pupils against bigger brutes and succeeded without doing much work.

In the Berrichon junior football team, back row, centre

'He was as disciplined as the other children in the class. In French he was above average, but in recitation, poetry and classics he was outstanding. He had read Molière and de Musset before he left. He also sang very well. But school didn't interest him.'

'I never felt I could fit in to the way it was run,' says Depardieu. 'I wanted to learn but I couldn't get into line like that, couldn't be regimented, as in the army.'

Instead he became star goalkeeper for the Berrichon junior football team. When the time came for the family to choose whether he should go to secondary education, there were no funds to buy books and school uniforms. But then Gérard didn't want to go anyway. He was in a hurry to do his own thing.

2

On the Road

1963, the year Kennedy was assassinated, was a momentous one for Gérard Depardieu. Still a boy in a man's body, he found a kind of freedom in himself. He kept up a cover of respectability by working as an apprentice in a printshop in the nearby rue Hôpitalière for something like £7 a month. Even in those days this was nothing and his earnings were massively augmented through co-operation with the GIs.

'The American GIs liked me,' he reminisces now, 'liked me a lot because I made myself useful. I'd get ration cards and buy bottles of whisky at the PX [the American Army and Air Force Exchange Services shops] for $1.50. Then I'd sell 'em on the streets for $4.00 and split the profits with the soldiers who'd got me the ration cards.'

With his best buddy Jacky Merveille, son of the manager of the local Crédit Agricole, who was later killed in a drink-driving crash on the bridge over the River Indre, he ran a profitable industry which operated around the clubs, like Le Cotton Club, Le Crazy, Le Lily, The Blue Lagoon and Jimmy's, opposite the prison, where the barmaid Suzanne apparently died from strangulation. Popular mythology says that if Jacky hadn't died Gérard would have gone to the bad but the truth is that Merveille's accident happened two years after Depardieu had left for Paris. Anyway, the GIs called Jacky 'Lemmy' after Lemmy Caution, the Eddie Constantine character, and Lemmy and Gégé – as they called Depardieu – were hardly regular goody two-shoes boys. At weekends they managed to get themselves into plenty of *mêlées* at country fairs and dances, and boredom drove them to

The prison in Châteauroux

do things that parents prefer their kids not to. The least troublesome of these was playing in a rock band which drove the neighbours mad.

These were the closing days of the Army of Occupation in France as de Gaulle took the country out of NATO and the eve of, many feared, France selling out to an ill-digested Americanisation: *le drugstore*, modern technology, new glitter for the old and (picturesquely) crumbling. France's post-war recovery and its belated industrialisation were racing ahead. The Algerian crisis was sapping the country of many of its young men and the Fifth Republic, with its constitution radically different from the Third and Fourth, was settling in uneasily.

As a bright kid, Depardieu knew that his future lay not in the printshop but elsewhere. Being a big chap and having always mixed with men older than himself, his experience had outstripped his age. At twelve he had been put on probation for either allegedly stealing cars – 'I learned to drive that way' – or stealing from cars, but again truth and myth are interwoven and nobody can remember which it was. A colleague of mine in Châteauroux thinks it was probably the former, as Depardieu, as a small boy, stole her friend's *vélosolex*.

One thing is for sure: following a fracas with the police, he spent a night

15

in the prison in the centre of Châteauroux, one street up from rue François Rabelais, named after a man he might not have heard of then but who was to become one of his heroes later.

'I felt I was free because I had no education and took what I wanted,' recalls Depardieu. 'Writers have tried to make this sound romantic but it was not. I stole cars, got into fights and spent time in police cells. The other children were already alcoholics and the only way to get their attention was to do bad things.

'If I had stayed with them, I, too, would have become an alcoholic and I am sure I would have got into a fight, lost control and killed somebody.

'By day, at the printshop, I'd dream, sitting by my *roto-imprimeuse* [printing press], watching the sheaves of paper come through, and knowing that I would soon leave,' he says. 'I knew there were bigger things. I'd read Jean Giono's lyrical communion with the earth, *Le Chant du Monde*, a book about horizons without boundaries. My head was already somewhere else.'

At around this time Depardieu had also started to focus on what ailed his family, the lack of emotion and ability to express feeling. He had become aware of more imaginative things in life than factory work, like books where emotions were spread across every page. Like most French kids surrounded by patriotism, he'd walked to school along roads named after Molière and Balzac, and sat drinking pop on benches in squares called Place Voltaire. From very early on, although he had difficulty reading, he says he was fascinated by words. Classmate Catherine Lison remembers his spouting French poetry in reams at school, which backs up headmaster Roger Lucas's reporting that the boy was transfixed by recitation.

Although he took part in school plays, young Depardieu's first real acting stints must have been using his persuasive powers to get the GIs who spoke no French to choose him rather than the dozen other kids who would procure goods for them. A friend of his, French TV's *Canal Plus* chatshow host Michel Denisot, who also grew up in Châteauroux and who worked with Gérard's sister Hélène on the local paper, told me that he remembers Depardieu quickly picking up enough American-English to fit in with the GIs easily.

'At twelve he was already a star. He was like Hercules and everybody called him Pétarou [from *pétard*, meaning 'firecracker']. You could see him any night in the striptease joints or cruising in the Buick convertibles. He was already acting his way through life.'

In an interview Depardieu told me that he actually credits his first acting efforts to improvising roles to get himself out of tight corners when apprehended by the law.

'You know how it is when you're young in a small town. It's like being a Jew. Even if you haven't done anything, they're always after you. Every time something got stolen the *gendarmes* used to come and look for me. "Come with us, Depardieu . . ." they'd say.'

He'd been quite a successful amateur welter-weight boxer at fourteen and, with his nose broken while working as a sparring partner for American Air Force men, was the sort of chap the police couldn't miss. Although his friend Pilorgé says that he was always very nervous and trembled with tension before a few rounds in the ring, his image was, and still is, one of a tough guy.

At thirteen he'd seen Molière's *Don Juan* performed on stage by Gabriel Monnet's company which had come from Bourges to Châteauroux. Even though he didn't get to grips with the play, the performance amazed him; and while it seemed ridiculous, that people would dress up and say funny words and go on stage to entertain others, the image remained.

'I'd sneak in through the props and come down from the wings when the lights went dark to sit in the theatre,' he recalls with his boyish giggle. 'For the first time I saw these people dressed up in disguise who had something quite extraordinary about them. I was astonished. It was rather like going into a château for the first time and finding that the people inside speak a different language. I'd never heard the language spoken like that. It was because of this play that I started to tell people later on that I was a drama student at the Théâtre Nationale Populaire, which was the only theatre place I'd ever heard of.'

Already addicted to the cinema, Depardieu found a world where emotions were allowed to survive. The cinema, however, also suited the delinquent identity he had chosen and it was a while before the formality of the theatre and he crossed tracks again.

'I've always felt *bien dans ma peau* [good in my skin] in the cinema. I saw all the American films, always sneaking in without paying and rushing to sit close up where you could really feel the moment when the white screen suddenly burst into life. I love Jean Marais's films. My idols were people like the between-the-war comedians Raimu and Bourvil, Michel Simon and Jean Marais. They could play any rubbish and it didn't matter.

'I also loved all the American gangster pictures, with Robert Mitchum and Burt Lancaster. And the Charles Laughton films! *Night of The Hunter — fantastique!* And of course, Westerns I'm really crazy about.

'At Châteauroux the gang never missed a thriller. I'd always identify with both the heroes and the baddies. We'd see a thriller, and then go out and try to imitate Mitchum or Cagney. We got our energy from them. From early on I wanted to be on screen, I wanted to be one of those guys with a gun in their belt or a sheriff's star on their lapels.

'But then I'm also a real *fleur bleue* [softie]. I like love stories and cry when they say goodbye. Like *Out of Africa* and *Gone With the Wind*, I like to be taken over by a film.

'Having come from a world where people didn't talk, to find people who had no difficulty in saying "I love you" was incredible. Much later I discovered Alfred de Musset and the classics properly. It was there that I really found words because these writers had no difficulty in saying something and they managed to say lots of different things at the same time.'

It was around then that this man who'd always walked alone wanted to belong.

'I knew I had to leave Châteauroux, to travel. I'd always hung around the station, watching people arrive, people leave. I wanted to see the sea again, although now I don't like the sea very much. The idea of flat sea and palm trees is not home. I like earth and greenery. But at that time I dreamed about the sea, at the printshop with my reams of paper.'

Already, he claims, he had left the family home to live with a couple of the sixty prostitutes then operating in Châteauroux. Most of them came down at weekends from Paris for the GIs but two young blondes, Irène and Michèle, lived on the edge of town near his beloved Bois de Belle-Isle, the forest with the lake north of the town. He remembers them as his real family, the one he always wanted to create for himself, an image caught up in his mind with excitement and violence, colourful life and rough times. Childhood, he feels, has no frontiers. It escapes time and space. 'Like sex,' he adds. His experience with Irène and Michèle taught him to use his freedom and live with anybody, anywhere.

'I was always playing the woman in relations with others. I was a child/adult. I had no protection, I was completely vulnerable. I had to seduce and charm people to keep going.'

Clearly, whether it was for a brief stint or a long one, the way he remembers it had an effect on his attitude to life.

'They took me in and treated me like a brother. I'd see them working all the time. I learned a lot early. All the prostitutes had a soft spot for me. I was a sort of minor gangster. I could have become a *really* bad boy. Nobody ever imposed any discipline on me.'

Irène gave him the tattoo of a star on his left wrist which was to remind him to always follow his own star. There are other tattoos, like the half inked-in heart above depicting love and hate, but they came later.

I went looking for Irène, who still lives in Châteauroux, and Michèle. My requests were greeted with some affront and a male friend who went prowling round the station at 2 am was laughed at loudly. Châteauroux hasn't had tarts since 1965, when the GIs left, somebody said. One now goes, it seems, to Bourges for them.

Defending himself in *Time* in 1991 Depardieu said that it would be 'perhaps accurate to say that I had sexual experiences at an early age'. Whether Depardieu served his sexual apprenticeship with Irène and Michèle doesn't really matter. Certainly when he left at fifteen to make his way in the world, he was no longer a virgin.

He hit the road, Kerouac-style. Heading for the RN 143, the road to Montluçon, hitchiking through La Châtre, where novelist George Sand had lived, he started his flight from childhood. He was bound for the Côte d'Azur. En route he lived rough, picking up work, odd jobs, selling things, jumping trains — a bum's ways and means. 'I half scared a woman to death on a train once,' he says. 'I was dirty and she looked down her nose at me. So I pulled a face, gave myself a tic and grinned horribly. Then I said: "Are you afraid?" and she screamed. It was my earliest little piece of cinema.' Finally he arrived at the coast, saw the serge-blue Mediterranean and decided to stay.

It was a coast he knew a little from his days with Le Berrichon Football Club as goalie for two years. Playing football, a game which in France holds the public with a paralysing popularity second only to Le Tour de France, meant going on tour. With the Berrichon team he'd defended goals all over France, as well as in Monte Carlo. Palm-lined *belle époque* seaside resorts were therefore not a total novelty and the Riviera seemed like a good place to start.

The beach that beckoned him most was La Garoupe, a small, secluded bay surrounded by pines with a restaurant and perfect view. Instantly struck by its beauty, he stopped and looked for work. A stone's throw from Nice and just round the corner from the Cap d'Antibes with its fabulous Hôtel du Cap, for three years the residence of Jules Verne, Depardieu found himself in a place that had everything Châteauroux could never have. Crawling with the rich and famous at play, the peninsula of Cap d'Antibes was and still is a jewel in the Med's crown. Now, when he returns to the Hôtel du Cap, it is as a celebrity at the Cannes Film Festival. Then, he used to sleep on the beach lulled, no doubt, by quantities of wine and the swing of the sea.

The beach, overlooked by a plateau with an amazing view across the Mediterranean, is a short boat-ride from the Iles d'Hyères where Jean-Luc Godard made *Pierrot Le Fou* with Belmondo in 1965. Depardieu admits that when he later saw the film he could never have imagined that he would inherit France's best-actor title from Belmondo although he might, at the time, have aspired to act for director Godard. (He was to act with Belmondo in 1974 in Alain Resnais' political thriller *Stavisky*, but so far has never done a film with Godard. He might, 'if we manage to see eye to eye'.)

La Garoupe, with its plateau of glorious gardens filled with exotic plants and ancient pensions and chapels, was an area so *recherché* that you had to be someone pretty special before they'd even serve you at the restaurant. Now La Garoupe is famous for Gérard Depardieu having been a *plagiste* (beachboy) there. Then it was famous for its exclusivity. It is one of the smallest beaches in the area, where the bodies sprawled elegantly on *transatlantiques* under parasols set out in prim rows in the sun were those of politicians, film stars and tycoons. Before the war Mistinguett had come to parade her beautiful legs on the sands. Greta Garbo and Marlene Dietrich had come too, and apparently de Gaulle, Churchill and Eisenhower had had lengthy lunchtime discussions there after the liberation of France.

'It was about twenty-five years ago,' reminisces Loulou, of Chez Joseph de la Garoupe. 'Gérard was only a lad, a splendid boy. He came for two seasons to be a beachboy here and the clients loved him. He had a wonderful way with people and he worked very hard raking the sand and looking after the customers.

'He came back to see us two or three times even when he was well into his career. But already when he was working with us we knew he wanted to be working in the theatre in Paris.'

When the season ended, and the final deckchair had been stored away and the beach raked for the last time before the winter winds took over, Depardieu packed up his beachtrunks and took off again. Tanned the colour of teak, his body primed like a side of beef at Les Halles, his hair striped blonde by days of sun and salt, it was time for the road.

He delights in telling how he got round much of Europe, *sans* passport, using a blind person's disability card he had somehow acquired. One of his more colourful tales is about hawking soap door to door, posing as a blind person with a white stick. With him came a tramp he'd picked up en

20

route, a man with a stump for an arm and a love of talking. The disabled pair, so he remembers, cut quite a dash.

The way he tells it, in his unconventional French with its intonation and laboured vowel sounds that are almost old-fashioned rural ('*un peu paysan nouveau*', his critics sometimes sneeringly call it), it sounds simply implausible. Just the kind of thing any aspiring actor would love to do, it was a lark that suited him down to the ground – entertaining, outrageous – and carried no social obligations, particularly in the 60s when anybody who was anybody had some sort of rackety background, like singers Johnny Hallyday and Serge Gainsbourg, who revelled in their lack of conformity.

It also gave him some groundwork for his first notable film role a decade later, as a washing-machine salesman in Marguerite Duras's film, *Nathalie Granger*.

3

To Paris

There are three versions of how in 1964 Depardieu got to Paris where he was to discover acting.

Some say the sixteen-year-old hitchhiked, others that his mother arranged for him to go there. *He* says he happened to be passing the station at Châteauroux, on a flash visit home from his walkabout, when he bumped into Michel Pilorgé, then a drama student. This version is the more colourful account and the one any studio would have printed in its press biography of a star. 'When truth and legend conflict, print the legend – it sells better and is more fun to read,' chortles a retired press officer from one of the Hollywood studios. 'In the old days we always created a bit of myth for our contract stars. So did the French. Godard started life fabricating bios of stars like Jayne Mansfield.'

According to one-time Gaumont bit-parter Depardieu, his introduction into the art happened when he saw 'Mimi' – his name for Pilorgé – standing on the platform at Châteauroux station.

'Where are you going?' Depardieu asked him.

'To Paris to work in the theatre,' Pilorgé replied, all neatly spruced up in a blue suit, white shirt and cravat.

Pilorgé was four years his senior and had already acted with François Simon in Geneva. This time he was studying acting at the Théâtre Nationale Populaire, France's most important post-war repertory company and the only one Depardieu had heard of. The younger man started asking about acting, about Paris, about where he lived. Pilorgé told him his family had a small flat there. He suggested he come along for the ride. Depardieu, having no cash, borrowed the fare off him and told some pals on the station to let his mother know he'd gone to Paris, probably until Sunday.

The train pulled out of the station with its graffiti, 'U.S. GO HOME', still scrawled on the station walls along with '*Algérie française*' and '*Défense de cracher*'. He says he knew, in his heart, that he was quitting for good. Speeding north through the flat greens and browns of crops and fields of the Cher, over the Loire at Orléans and into the ugly industrial sprawl of satellites of the capital, the 265 kilometres between Châteauroux and Paris passed quickly. It is not one of France's most impressive train routes. The left bank is filled by the spread of 60s highrises, the right with industrial deco warehouses, along with the Seine and her boats working on the murky brown water. It isn't special now but then it must have been particularly desolate.

To arrive at Austerlitz Station on Place Valhubert is probably the least heart-stopping of all the Paris arrivals. A grubby concrete and stained-steel structure built after the war, possibly the greatest significance it was to hold for the aspiring actor was that in 1976, playing a young unemployed provincial in the controversial *Maîtresse*, he would arrive in Paris from the sticks at Austerlitz. (Coincidentally, his friend from Châteauroux was also in the film.)

Pilorgé took him to the apartment, owned by his father, the local doctor in Châteauroux. An unremarkable two-roomer at the top of a building in rue de la Glacière, now quite a nice part of the 13th *arrondissement*, it was a regular 60s student pad. There were three or four others already living there, something that didn't particularly surprise the provincial teenager. The fact that they were doing their own cooking, however, did, and that they had *proper* conversations amazed him. They might have been living on the smell of an oil-rag and surviving on sandwiches made from long *ficelles* and chunky *baguettes* with a hint of pâté or sliver of ham, but they used their endless energy to talk and compare and spend hours discussing theories, approaches, attitudes.

'It was a totally different life from the one I'd known,' he says, still apparently surprised. 'Here were people who read a lot. They'd already read all the books I'd been told to read but never had. They discussed their lectures together, wrote poetry, novels, planned great projects... I was fascinated. It was like coming out of a stupor. I heard people saying out loud, in broad daylight, things that I'd been feeling for years.

'I didn't know how to talk, to converse. I'd come from a background where people didn't talk. It had engendered a kind of violence in me which is perhaps OK when you're young and you can turn into a delinquent, but it gets very heavy when you're older. I needed to talk.

'I'd spent years on my own talking to myself, talking to the trees. Because I was alone so much as a kid I lost my speech. I couldn't finish a sentence, I was completely incoherent. I could talk, yes, but it was like . . .' He opens his mouth and makes grunting noises. When he gets fired up and animated now he still talks in great gushes, seldom finishing a sentence properly.

'In Paris, people communicated. Suddenly I found, for the first time, that I was able to say lots of different things. People would listen, we would talk, sitting in cafés drinking coffee.'

Courtesy of Pilorgé, Depardieu did not return to Châteauroux the following Sunday. The self-styled hoodlum who loved the mythology of acting a part was going to try for his biggest role, breaking the mould and actually doing it. With his knapsack full of jumbled emotions, deceptively burly chest and broad sloping shoulders, *that* nose and the luminous, deep-set, greyish eyes, sometimes dark as thunder, he was going to start from scratch and put himself about in the market place as a performer. Almost overnight he became quiet as he paddled around in the shallows, way out of his depth.

The world outside now saw the start of the violent anti-de Gaulle street riots, the arrival of tens of thousands of Algerian settlers, *les pieds noirs* (who had begun to return as refugees after Algeria's independence in 1962), the first rumblings of the Paris student revolt, Beatlemania. For Depardieu, all were to pass unnoticed. He merely mentions going down to the student barricades in the Sorbonne riots in May 1968 'for a laugh'.

The morning after his arrival, Depardieu went along with the others to lectures at the TNP. Nobody seemed to mind when, as one of the gang, he slid into the class of Charles Dullin, an actor who, like so many others (including the great lion of French theatre, Louis Jouvet), was putting something back into the industry by nurturing the new generation. The TNP, now the Théâtre Nationale de Chaillot, is an exceptional company with a drama school attached. Generally considered to have transformed French theatre to what it is now, it was started in 1920 by the actor Firmin Gémier in the Trocadéro Palace. Designed as a touring company, it took all kinds of productions around France, training young performers as it went. Jean Vilar was a mainstay and leading actors like Gérard Philipe were regular members of the cast. Jack Lang, now France's Minister of Culture, headed it up in the early 70s. To date more than 1,500 actors, from Philippe Noiret to Maria de Medeiros of the American film *Henry and June*, have gone through the TNP.

Teaching at the TNP in 1964 were some of France's top classical drama coaches like Jean-Laurent Cochet, Jean-Pierre Darras and Georges Riquier. They were impressed by this uncouth, yet withdrawn boy, with nails bitten to the quick, who didn't try to hide his proletarian origins or unclassical features. They cautiously took him on as a student and, owing to his circumstances, charged no fee. He signed up for all the courses and attended every lesson, furiously taking notes but hiding them so the others wouldn't see his bad handwriting.

Cochet, who gave him a formal and imperiously classical apprenticeship as a drama student, comments: 'I saw in this boy a complete lack of culture but an awakening intelligence and a real passion for the theatre. He was tied in knots, even incapable of finishing sentences without blasting the words out and he blocked completely when in the company of three people. The emotional charge was too violent for him.' (One of Depardieu's more melodramatic and most quoted remarks − 'Acting saved me, otherwise I would have become a killer' − is perhaps more accurate than it seems.) This didn't prevent Cochet from giving Depardieu, for his first night's homework, extracts from Albert Camus's *Caligula* to prepare for an audition the following day as a test to join his drama class. Bolstered by being told that Caligula was a mad Roman emperor and should be treated that way, something he could go along with even though he couldn't understand the things he said or did, Depardieu spent the night learning the words, then in his nervousness broke a chair on stage.

'I was dumb from hyperemotion. I was so frightened, terrified that I wouldn't be able to say my words, frightened that I wouldn't be able to remember them. Everybody must have felt this tension. Finally whatever it was became unblocked and I passed into the light.

'Afterwards Cochet took me into his office and told me I'd passed and that I would play Pyrrhus in his production of *Caligula*.'

It was the first of many triumphs.

For nine months he followed courses there, a routine he considers his 'time of gestation'. He agonised over texts − refusing to change so much as a comma − because half the time he didn't understand them.

'I learned the texts because I've got a good memory but I never understood what I was declaiming. I used to feel hot when I heard certain speeches but mainly I heard words like a complete innocent. I didn't know what they meant but there was an imagery, an instinctive feeling for the ideas. I felt I had a personal communication with writers like Molière and Racine and de Musset. I didn't understand them but their imagery meant something. Initially the versification was a burden. It was through prose that I came to understand verse.

'I suppose, because I was charged with these ideas, these images, it was natural for me to go into the cinema, but then I just wanted to be the angry young man of the theatre! No, that's not entirely true. I never dreamed of being an actor. I just wanted to amuse myself and discover lots of things.'

Declaiming and throwing his body and soul into the role infused it with a tantalising energy which the TNP had not seen before. He was their instant star pupil, and they cast him in more and more ambitious roles. Within his first month he was playing second lead as the impossible Don Cesar de Bazan in Victor Hugo's *Ruy Blas*. Beginning to feel better in this new environment where he lived and breathed culture, his confidence grew, balancing his insecurity with the new forces. Acting was his own form of therapy.

'I learnt to be in the light,' he recalls. 'The stage is like a cage of light. People are no longer afraid of you – they are the ones out there in the dark, watching.'

Depardieu's inability to express himself, what he calls his 'loss of words', has always been cited as a key trauma in his life and at the TNP he started to sort it out with the help of a professor who specialised in speech therapy. He was Alfred Tomatis and all students were expected to attend his clinic for a free audiometric test. Tomatis found that young Gérard's ear was, literally, too sensitive – his hearing was too acute. He'd listen to music, and somehow the ear took in too much information and scrambled it up. 'I was such a mess that my words started crashing into each other and made no sense. I couldn't finish a sentence. It was only the words and texts of others that helped me back to a vocabulary.' He worked with Tomatis for five or six months developing a phenomenal memory and learning how to speak properly. It was, Depardieu recalls, like a second birth.

During that time he also met a fellow student called Elisabeth Guignot. A gorgeous woman, rather in the Bardot mould but with wavy brown hair, she was the daughter of an executive of the Paris Métro. Seven years his senior, she was studying mime and psychology, and attending the course as part of her thesis, which was on the body in space. Jean-Laurent Cochet, who normally didn't enthuse over individual students, spoke of her with great respect. Working near her in class Depardieu always found himself gravitating towards her. With her, he writes touchingly in *Lettres Volées*, he ceased to feel deaf, stopped being enclosed. 'You spoke to me in such a way that I heard everything.' Of him she said: 'Somebody totally new appeared and performed de Musset like I'd never heard it before.' It was an attraction of opposites; he was sixteen, she twenty-three.

Elisabeth helped him with his incoherence, taught him how to read the classics and showed him how to understand their sense. Reading authors like de Musset and Marivaux, he says, cast enduring shafts of light on his attitude to the classics, which he still adores.

'The words that really cleared the blockage for me were from de Musset's "On ne badine pas avec l'amour", the passage that begins "*Trouvez-vous à midi à la petite fontaine*". Those words, that speech, they take you out of yourself.'

Depardieu became almost obsessed with de Musset, who wrote of the delights and desperation of love as he had experienced them for a time as George Sand's lover, just around the corner from Châteauroux.

Depardieu tells of how he enquired of his friends where he could find de Musset. He wanted to talk to him. They gave him the address of Père Lachaise, the cemetery in which de Musset's imposing tomb stands. Depardieu leapt on his *vélosolex* and headed north to the forty-four-acre home of 100,000 graves. Apparently he laughed when he realised the joke but nevertheless strode up the hill from Boulevard Diderot, past the beds of tulips, past the graves of Colette and Rossini on the left, to his hero. He says he still goes back to commune with the gaunt, handsome statue of the poet. Now he also visits Molière, Balzac, Proust and Apollinaire; but at that point he'd probably never heard of them.

4

Nose to the Grindstone

In the 60s France's cinematic Nouvelle Vague had just crested the wave and a character like Gérard Depardieu, teenager, was ideal fodder for *cinema vérité* café society. Here was a sophisticated peasant, submissive sex symbol, boy wonder raging with savage but naive talent *and* from the 'other' sector of the population – not the affluent, artistic, educated one. In short, he was a perfect *ingénu* who struck a chord with French people brought up to conform but dying to break out of the system.

He had hardly finished his studies when he bumped into a friend at a café called, symbolically, Le Dédé, opposite the Ecole Polytechnique, just around the corner from where he was living.

'*Tiens*, Pétar,' she said, using one of his Châteauroux nicknames, 'my cousin is looking for a beatnik to act in his film.'

Her cousin was film director Roger Leenhardt. She took her friend over to his apartment and the two men got along famously. It was only going to be a short but it would be his first contact with the camera, with a fee of 500 francs a day for two days to play a character not entirely dissimilar to himself. A time was fixed for Depardieu to be on set the next day but he overslept. Leenhardt went out and bought him an alarm clock. They started again.

The filming went well, Depardieu wasn't required to do much except hang around smoking in a café, playing a bearded yob who represented the don't-give-a-damn society. He looked fine but had to be dubbed as his words were inaudible. It was called *Le Beatnik et le Minet* (in slang '*minet*' means both 'dandy' and 'fanny') and when it wrapped he went off to do another summer as a deckchair attendant on the Côte d'Azur, this time at the Cannes Plage des Sports, where he was to return when his films were shown in competition at the film festival.

Returning to Paris at the end of the season he heard from Elisabeth that Agnès Varda, a director who made films about the fringes of society, was also looking for a hippyish character for her new film. It was 1967, the Paris hippy was in and the film was *Christmas Carol*. He remembers not even having to change his clothes for the role, and saying lines like: 'Why bother to work? I get my money from begging.'

Depardieu did everything from carrying the camera to cooking the lunch. Although the film was never completed and he was never paid, it was hands-on experience. Then, somehow, a photo of Depardieu landed on the right desk when they were casting a TV serial called *Rendezvous à Badenberg*. He'd hardly finished a small role in a forgettable theatrical production when he found himself playing the leading man in a neat little love story. It was nothing special but the well-known actor-director, Rufus, was also involved in the project. A man of great influence in French dramatic circles, he took Depardieu with him to Le Café de la Gare, Paris's most fashionable café-theatre near the Hôtel de Ville, a few streets away from the then unbuilt Pompidou Centre.

Le Café de la Gare, a wildly innovative company with its ramshackle theatre set at the back of a cobbled courtyard, was the seeding ground for dozens of struggling young Paris actors. It was there he met comedian Patrick Dewaere and actress Miou-Miou, his future partners in several movies, particularly Bertrand Blier's outrageous *Les Valseuses*, the film that was to hurl him into the public eye in 1974.

Although he hated the improvisation needed for the mad fun and lightning responses of café-theatre, he stayed for six months.

'I didn't like it very much because I was a bit far removed from all that. I didn't have that sort of touch, I wasn't a Parisian. I was still a hoodlum from the provinces. And I didn't like to improvise. I'm still incapable of it. I find it easier to say the words of others than make up my own.'

Some of his unease towards open-ended revue and stand-up work must have been ingrained during his formal background at the TNP. Traditionally most stage actors despised the cinema and loathed the irreverence of send-up and improvisation.

'But in café-theatre we had fun together. I learned a lot about myself and my abilities. Patrick, Miou-Miou and I even made a short film called

Le Café de la Gare Theatre, Paris

La Vie Sentimentale de George le Tueur [*The Love Life of Killer George*] which was outrageous.'

A gross but biting little film in which Depardieu plays a desperate husband with three kids and a wife he can't leave, he's shorn and besuited, with eyes large and dramatic, and overacting like mad. He ends up running around half naked in a torn shirt, very indicative of what was to come in future films.

At that stage of his career he might have preferred the theatre and the classics to the cinema but he took whatever work he could get. Between 1967 and 1971 he did nine plays, including *Boys in the Band* directed by his old tutor Cochet, played in drag in a French version of Terence Frisby's *There's a Girl In My Soup*, acted in *L'inconnu* and *Galapagos* with Nathalie Baye, his co-star years later in films *Le Retour de Martin Guerre* and *Rive Droite Rive Gauche*. There were also bits and pieces of TV work, including an episode in the *Maigret* series.

Baye recalls those early days: 'I was very young, still at the Conservatoire, when I met Gérard on *Galapagos*. It was a difficult play, not an entirely happy set, but he made me relax by making me laugh. He has this incredible ability to make people laugh, which means that one gets on with the work quicker. Gérard is a man who has no time to lose. He's capable of making three films at once. Sometimes I find his enormous energy almost frightening.

'We got to know each other well on *Galapagos* and have regularly worked together since then. He is one of the few actors with whom I've remained friends outside work.'

In 1971 and 1972 Depardieu appeared in tiny roles in seven feature films. The first, poetically entitled *Le Cri du Cormoran le Soir au-dessus des Jonques*, starred Bernard Blier (father of director Bertrand) and Jean Carmet, an actor who became a friend and mentor. A Gaumont production of Eva Hunter's light novel about smuggling diamonds, Depardieu plays a killer complete with gun, hat and impeccable grey suit.

Carmet, one of France's most beloved of actors, was first dazzled by Depardieu on a Paris stage when Gérard was nineteen.

'He was already stunning, even then thoroughly commanded the stage. In his mouth the worst banalities became poetry. On stage, he flowers. Wherever he is, that is where the action begins.' Old enough to be Depardieu's father, Carmet is small and mild. Together now they look like Laurel and Hardy.

The next film was *Un Peu de Soleil dans L'Eau Froide* from Françoise

Sagan's novel with Depardieu playing Claudine Auger's brother, an insignificant role. Ringo Starr's wife Barbara Bach, then an unknown actress from Germany, also starred.

1972 was to be his year as a typecast extra – or *utilité* – in films best forgotten. He played yet another young besuited thug in *Le Viager*, a film directed by Pierre Tchernia and co-starring Carmet, and in Denys de la Patellière's *Le Tueur* he was a 'grass' called Fredo. Hardly name-in-lights stuff, it was nonetheless solid apprenticeship, as Depardieu was working with the backbone of European screen talent. One of his role models and certainly the French actor he has been most compared to, Jean Gabin, played *Le Tueur*'s lead, a police commissioner, and like Carmet, Gabin became a sort of godfather to the volatile fledgling. Then there was José Giovanni's *La Scoumoune*, where he had another walk-on part as a member of the underworld, this time with the actor whose popularity he was to inherit, Jean-Paul Belmondo, in the lead.

1973 started with *Au Rendezvous de la Mort Joyeuse*, a Franco-Italian co-production directed by Juan Buñuel. With a crashing Beethoven soundtrack, he was Beretti, a man faced with bizarre happenings and little else. Next was *L'Affaire Dominici*, with Jean Gabin. Directed by Claude Bernard-Aubert, a journalist who covered a murder called the 'Dominici Affair' and concerning the triple murder of three English campers in 1952 in Provence, Depardieu played a young peasant called Zézé. The role, for him, was a doddle but he was beginning to tire of bit parts. Then came *Nathalie Granger*.

While he was working on stage between his bit parts he had appeared in a play by British playwright Edward Bond called *Saved*. Claude Régy was directing and breaking new ground, as it was a very violent piece.

'I needed very young, very athletic actors and somebody told me about Gérard,' says Régy. 'I went to see him at the Gaîté-Montparnasse where he was playing a fisherman. He had such a presence about him that I engaged him instantly.

'One night Marguerite [the distinguished writer Duras], who was adapting David Storey's two-hander *Home*, came to a rehearsal, saw this unruly giant bursting with energy, and immediately asked him – demanded of him – to be in her film *Nathalie Granger*, co-starring Jeanne Moreau.'

Depardieu tackled *Home* (at less than half the age of the original actors, John Gielgud and Ralph Richardson) with Michel Lonsdale the next season before shooting started on *Nathalie Granger*.

'I had never seen anything like him,' says Duras. 'Natural genius,

Conversation with Marguerite Duras

incredible intelligence and completely unspoiled. He didn't dare talk in those days. I'm not sure he knew how to read and write. During the filming, Jeanne Moreau said: "I wonder where Marguerite found a Shakespearean actor?" She felt that dimension right away.'

'It was one of the most important encounters of my career,' says Depardieu, 'because after *Nathalie Granger* there was *La Femme du Gange, Le Camion* and *Baxter, Vera Baxter.*'

The role, an adolescent one, required him to do a ten-minute cameo as an ominous washing-machine salesman trying to sell his wares to Jeanne Moreau at the country home of Nathalie Granger.

'She actually told me that François Perrier [now one of Depardieu's best acting buddies] had already said "no" to it. "*Ah, bon,*" was what I said,' he comments of the role. 'When she was explaining it to me I wasn't really listening because I was thinking of my mother who was always taken in by salesmen in their nice suits selling her useless things that she couldn't afford to pay for. She'd sign on the dotted line and then these things would arrive. It was a disaster. I was also thinking of when I was a door-to-door salesman. I'd work with a pal and I'd keep the housewife busy at the front door while my pal was stealing chickens in the back yard.'

Nathalie Granger is a curious, somewhat intellectual film about a family, the Grangers, who live in a country house with a nameless woman (Moreau). Against a background of domestic life, you hear on the radio news of a couple of young killers in the region. At this point the salesman arrives.

'I said yes, of course. Marguerite is one of those directors for whom work is part of life. She is an amazing woman, a monster. When she said, "Come to my house tomorrow morning", I thought that we would first discuss the part. I walked in and we started shooting there and then. I couldn't believe it. Working with Marguerite is like working with the earth ... the situation is the weather with the actors as the seasons.'

Depardieu's performance of a man who is physically impressive but psychologically vulnerable caught the public eye. Critic Jean de Baroncelli in *Le Monde* wrote: 'It's a good part and the way he tackles it reveals an original talent.' Robert Chazal in *France-Soir* said: 'He gives an absolutely first-class performance as the commercial traveller: no doubt the start of a fine career.' Chazal went on to chart this career in a book, *Gérard Depardieu – l'autodidacte inspiré*, in 1982.

Of Jeanne Moreau, who clearly bowled Depardieu over, he said at the time that before he met her she'd represented to him just a mouth, hair and a voice – particularly a voice. 'Working with her I found that she had everything. She was a great influence on my early work.' They were to work together again, fifteen months later, in *Les Valseuses*, Depardieu's breakthrough film.

In the intervening months he packed in three more films, setting a pattern of three films a year that he has managed consistently for nearly two decades. One was back with director José Giovanni, who employed him again in a small role as an ubiquitous member of the underworld in his Jean Gabin–Alain Delon bank-robber flick, *Deux Hommes dans la Ville*. Delon, who was the producer, saw the film as a judgement on society and on a bad prison system. Depardieu doubted that but was happy to play the role.

Another was *Rude Journée pour la Reine* (*Hard Day for the Queen*) which, out of the blue at a press conference in 1990 in Los Angeles, he announced was his favourite film. This was a surprise, as his role as Fabien can be missed in a blink or two, but the film, a touching and thoughtful tapestry made up of wild strands of relationships, definitely stands on its own in the light of its leading lady, Simone Signoret. The late wife of Yves Montand, it was she who, years later, was responsible for suggesting

Depardieu play what, in 1990, became his most popular role, in the film of Marcel Pagnol's novel *Jean de Florette*. (In *Rude Journée*, Depardieu actually acts with Orane Demazis, who had been married to Pagnol.) A further link was meeting a man who was to become Depardieu's best friend in the industry, Yves Montand's nephew Jean-Louis Livi, who was first his agent through the influential actors' agency in Paris, Artmedia, and is now the producer of most of his films.

The third film was *Les Gaspards*, with Jean Carmet and Philippe Noiret. Both have become close friends of Depardieu's. With Carmet, the man with the used face and traditional 'Frenchman' appearance, he made dozens of films; with Noiret, he made *Fort Saganne* and *Uranus*. *Les Gaspards* would have been his first substantial role but as he was scheduled to start work on *Les Valseuses* a month later, cuts had to be made to his part. Set in the Latin Quarter, Gérard, now twenty-four, played a local postman and wine merchant whose supplies are regularly raided. The postman wasn't a sign from above of things to come but the wine-selling angle certainly was, as he now owns a château encircled by vineyards in Anjou that produces a selection of fine wines.

Les Gaspards was directed by Pierre Tchernia and is about a bookseller (Michel Serrault) who investigates a curious underground phenomenon. A forerunner of the mutant ninja turtles, it turns out that a group of noble anarchists are living in splendour in subterranean Paris. Called 'Les Gaspards', they are led by Noiret and do all kinds of marvellous things underground like grow mushrooms and have chamber music concerts.

When the Americans bought the US distribution rights to the film they had difficulty with the title translation. *Gaspards* literally means 'rats'. To avoid unwarranted horror-pic connotations they screened it as *The Holes*, which sounds almost as unsavoury.

5

Les Valseuses

Depardieu has often said that without the love and patience of Elisabeth Guignot there wouldn't be a Gérard Depardieu, actor. Although reported to be an inflammable, at times on/off marriage, friends say he can't live without her. He says if he lost her he'd be totally handicapped and wouldn't know what to do. Some even say she was the mother he had always longed for. Other people's marriages are always a matter of speculation to outsiders but whatever the truth of this one, it was, at the time, a meeting of souls. He's always called his life with Elisabeth, which certainly has had its ups and downs, 'a work of love'.

She was from a middle-class family with roots in the Jura region of France and still calls herself a *terrienne* (someone who loves the earth). From the minute they met in Cochet's class, says Gérard, they have been together, living a sort of picaresque life that the French press has cherished and lovingly reproduced in 'perfect couple' pictures. Elisabeth always looks like a model, Gérard the devoted husband.

In a touching letter to her, he writes of how although he is still unable to plunge easily into his emotions to say 'I love you', the thing he considers the most important in the world he *can* say: 'I love her.' 'So, my Elisabeth,' he writes, 'between you and me, I'm going to tell you a secret: "I love her, I love her for always, forever".'

Tender stuff for the Gallic hulk, but no less genuine for that. Depardieu's spirit is charming, his heart generous. He is eccentric but never mannered, one of the few showbiz personalities who doesn't pander to their position of power. His wife says he plays the game; when he's treated like a star he behaves like one. As a couple, they prefer not to be put to the test in public.

He was twenty-one when he married her in 1970. It was an improbable marriage; it didn't fit the macho image. It suggested rather a boy finally admitting his need of a family, an anchor. They were living in a tiny apartment in rue Lepic, a long, shady street full of little shops and old-world charm at the edge of Montmartre. Pigalle is at one end, Sacré Coeur at the other, and it was the sort of place two emerging young 'must-sees' should have been in.

Both were working, buzzing on his mobylette between television studios, theatres and occasional films without skipping a beat. He nostalgically recounts returning to rue Lepic at three in the morning and leaving again at seven 'with the verve of a new-born baby'. Having made a real home had given him new energy and a sense of security. Conforming for the first time in his life to some sort of domestic routine represented continuity.

Then they had a baby, son Guillaume, and the balance started to shift.

'With my first child I felt that I'd passed a headland,' says Depardieu. 'I finally knew where I was going.'

For Elisabeth it was less of a straight course. After partnering her husband in some pre-runs for *Saved* at the TNP theatre at Chaillot she came home one night to find a maggot in Guillaume's bottle. 'I cracked and knew I had to decide to give up the theatre.' There was no choice about it. Her husband was building a strong working relationship with director Claude Régy, who was always prospecting for new talent and loved Depardieu's ability to 'understand instinctively and interpret physically'. The man who got Harold Pinter and Edward Bond known in France, Régy represented the leader Depardieu was looking for. The two of them did five plays together. The only alternative for Elisabeth was to sacrifice their footloose life in Montmartre for that of the wife and mother in a dreary flat by the Porte de Vanves, one of the soulless, grey outer areas of Paris that Aristide Bruand had sung of so plaintively. Daughter Julie arrived just when *Les Valseuses* started its shoot in August 1973.

Two years before, director Bertrand Blier had noticed Depardieu playing the part of a mentally retarded man at the Théâtre de la Madeleine when he had gone to see his father Bernard perform in *Galapagos*. Blier Junior then followed the career of Depardieu, a man ten years younger, with particular interest. He'd worked in films as a director and was eager to write something reflective of the changing times, marking a progression

Paris's model couple: Elisabeth and Gérard

from the New Wave, many of whose directors had developed middle-aged spread, into the permissive 70s. Like many, he criticised the fact that the New Wave often neglected modern French issues by using the director's own vision of reality, often more an inner than a socio-political one.

Blier's first book, the 420-page *Les Valseuses* (translated into English under the title of *Making It*), was published in 1972. It was *un succès fou* among those wanting change, as it offended all the niceties of the bourgeoisie, toppled taboos and spiked every sacred cow in Georges Pompidou's tightly buttoned France. The bourgeoisie, particularly the female of the species, were horrified. It came out at a time when French society was on the point of a little lid-blowing. In America, the Nixon corruption scandal was about to break with Watergate; Britain was plunging into heady strikes and a three-day week, and equality was being promised to women workers.

Meanwhile Depardieu, not quite sure what his part in this movement for change should be but determined to be in it, was associating with Régy and other controversial directors; a vogue for the works of Austro-German/British playwrights had hit France, and it was they who were providing French actors with meaty subjects and strong roles that related to the modern world in a time of boringly safe revivals of French plays. Depardieu was getting good reviews, mainly along the 'sensitive wild beast tamed' and 'unedited charm' lines, and had already won the Grand Prix Gérard Philipe as most promising newcomer. When Blier came to him with his script about two 'giggling layabouts, natural grandsons of Rabelais and Guignol', he naturally accepted. After ten films – he was about to spend a week shooting *Les Gaspards* – he was still waiting for the big break.

Respected director Maurice Pialat had asked him to be in *La Gueule Ouverte*, a study of a woman dying of cancer at home, but it was a script that represented everything he was trying to avoid. On top of that he found that Pialat was a man living on a different plane. They were to make three films together, but in the mid-70s the time was right for the Blier film.

'*Les Valseuses* was a quicker form of communication. Instinctively I knew it would work. Blier's words are so strong. They are like de Musset's, real words. The only difficulty with real words is that they sound dirty and the audience doesn't like that!' He giggles his upwardly rolling giggle – the latent schoolboy within. (When he laughs it always ends up as a cross between water burbling down the plughole and a chuckle, rather like the laugh he later has with Andie MacDowell during the rooftop photo sessions in *Green Card*.) 'I leapt in with both feet. Jean-Claude [his character] was a guy who never wanted to be bored, who wanted to live a thousand

Patrick Dewaere, Miou-Miou and Depardieu scandalising the bourgeoisie in Les Valseuses, *1974*

different emotions and flat out at a hundred mph. That's what I wanted too, we all did. But we knew we had to break rules to do it.'

Blier contacted the Café de la Gare team, Dewaere and Miou-Miou. He rounded up his friend Jeanne Moreau and some young hopefuls, including Isabelle Huppert and Brigitte Fossey. He persuaded Stéphane Grappelli to do the music and an unknown Dutch cameraman, Bruno Nuytten, filmed it. Michel Pilorgé played a man on a motorbike.

Les Valseuses (released as *Making It* in the UK and *Going Places* in the USA) broke French box-office records and made instant stars of the three leads – more so of the two men, as very few actresses had been seen doing comedy with no clothes on in mainstream films before. Jeanne Moreau was chastised by American women for being in such a dirty movie. Brigitte Fossey was severely criticised for being in a scene that involved breastfeeding on a train. Over France's favourite child star, Isabelle Huppert, then only eighteen, seen in the film having sex at the side of the road with both men, hands came up in shock and shame.

At the time, it was all too *monstrueux* for words. And the words! No film had used dialogue that went along such explicit lines, as when Jean-Claude drops off Marie-Ange from his (stolen) car and asks to touch her fanny for luck. 'I never heard that brought good luck,' she giggles. 'Oh, sure,' says Jean-Claude. 'Touching something dirty always brings good luck. Like stepping in shit.'

The first time I saw it, at the Rex Cinema in Avignon in 1974, I tottered out rigid with shock. I was living in the Vaucluse and had gone all the way to Avignon especially to see it because I'd heard from French friends that it was *un film vachement formidable*. In the days when '*vachement*' was still an intensifying adverb which truly strengthened a statement, I was primed with anticipation. They were sure I'd love it. I was *une britannique*, so I must come from Dr Spock's permissive society. I also had no job (I was doing cropwork on local farms) and therefore was, at heart, tarred with the same brush as the travelling trio, *les valseuses*. The word '*valseuses*', they added chortling and indicating their crotches, meant 'testicles'.

A story of society's corrupt effect on youth, it is about two men, Jean-Claude and Pierrot, and a shampooist called Marie-Ange, who rob and fornicate their way through France. It was not, in a country that had traditionally reflected its society in its films, 'typically French', with its multiple scenes of sexual activity and vandalism. However, the sight of such blatant on-screen loutishness and promiscuity in those still (comparatively) prudish days didn't actually stir me; what impressed me was Gérard Depardieu. For many, like me, who hadn't heard of him, it was his brazen nudity that hit home; deeper than that, there was a salty sexuality and raw animal presence, coupled with pure innocence and *joie de vivre*, that added up to a mesmerising actor. He was definitely *not* 'typically French'. There was none of the archetypical boudoir Frenchman Charles Boyer-style or the quirky *je m'en foutisme* of Belmondo or the elegance of Delon. Depardieu's earthiness and bravado were simply stunning. The film was leagues ahead of its time. Now, seeing *Les Valseuses* again, shock thresholds have obviously changed and people come away smiling comfortably about it.

Blier had made the right choice for his robustly realistic story of Jean-Claude and Pierrot. The film follows their progress from the point when they decide to 'borrow' a lovely new Citroën to burn around in. When they return the vehicle to the spot they took it from its outraged owner, a kinky hairdresser, he greets them with a gun in his hand. Still, they manage to take his girlfriend, Marie-Ange (Miou-Miou), and the car, and flee. In the escape Pierrot is wounded in the groin. They find a doctor, who has

Depardieu on the throne: Les Valseuses

to put a stitch in his testicle, as that's where he's been hit. On the way out they pinch the doctor's wallet. Pierrot then becomes obsessed with the idea that he has lost his virility – bad news as sex is virtually his only activity in life.

Already on parole for a previous offence and leaving Marie-Ange in Paris, they decide to hole up in an out-of-season seaside resort and break into an empty villa. Quickly bored, they return to Paris to collect Marie-Ange and discover that Pierrot's fears are unfounded. (This is one of the best screen sex scenes ever, as Blier shoots it with great humour, largely from the angle of the pumping rump, panning in to Miou-Miou who lies there, frigid as an iceberg, counting the flies on the ceiling.) The story roams on to introduce Jeanne Moreau, a long-term prisoner on parole, with whom they have a wonderful time before she shoots herself, leaving only letters from her prisoner son Jacques (Jacques Chailleux), who is due for release.

Jacques and Marie-Ange get it together, Marie-Ange finally and deliriously having a climax with him, which rather puts the noses of her two travelling companions out of joint. When funds run short, Jacques, with Jean-Claude and Pierrot, raids the house of his prison warden but things don't go to plan. They find the nest egg but shoot the warden. Once more on the run, they come across a family picnicking by a river. As the *valseuses*'s car is low on petrol, they take not only the family's compliant daughter (Huppert) but their Citroën too.

The critics found *Les Valseuses* '*une véritable révélation*'. *Paris-Match*, house journal of the bourgeoisie, called it 'colourful' and 'truthful' with 'a rare quality – it makes one feel happy'. Labelled as a sort of hymn for youth in France, more people went to see it than to *The Sting* or *The Man With the Golden Gun*. At the time it ranked second only to *Emmanuelle*. (In Britain it was refused a general certificate by the censors and the film was only allowed a limited release in Greater London.)

Depardieu remembers it all as huge fun, but always with an edge. He recalls Blier, one of his closest friends – 'Blier is family' – arriving on set each morning with his briefcase in hand, pipe in mouth, very austere and shy, introverted and saying little while he (Depardieu) and Dewaere chaffed around insolently like two naughty schoolboys, uneasy with so much focus being put on them, yet revelling in being buddies doing something meaningful and controversial. Their youthful friendship forged in café-theatre was warmly reflected throughout the film, particularly in the bathroom scene when Pierrot and Jean-Claude talk together about home. The gangly Dewaere, like Depardieu a frank and instinctive actor, had also come

Buddies and voyous *together: Dewaere and Depardieu*

from an imperfect background and the two ran parallel careers, until Dewaere committed suicide in 1982.

Both always considered *Les Valseuses* a highly effective stone hurled through the window of French cinema. It was their attempt in life to do something to an over-stylised society full of long-standing taboos. Thumbing their noses at French uptightness right where it hurt most, with their flagrant nudity and spontaneous gestures, both of them, as boyish, insecure products of that society, needed little encouragement to use the world as their stage. Blier's film *was* one huge game and if the story didn't fit, they made it up with personal anecdotes and live action.

'Blier was only thirty-two when he made this film, and it was very hard for him because Patrick and I were young, stupid boys,' laughs Depardieu. 'One day the producer had to go and get him out of jail because he'd hit the tiles in desperation, got drunk and ended up in a fight.'

Depardieu and Dewaere were often partnered as the wild boys of the screen, hand in glove on screen and off, and they lived up to their reputation royally. Much of it simply concerned basic life and coping with it. Depardieu recounts in *Lettres Volées* how, one night at the location hotel of *Les Valseuses,* he heard moans and groans coming from a room nearby while

44

he was 'trying to find sleep while masturbating'. Suddenly his door flew open and Dewaere stood there in a terrible state of distress.

'I thought Miou-Miou was in bed making love with you,' he gasped, in tears, completely demented.

'You were drowning in a chapter of *Les Valseuses*,' Depardieu wrote in his 'stolen letter' to Dewaere, 'completely confused between life and acting. You couldn't handle the tough side of it. You were too sensitive.'

6

Naked Ambition

Depardieu, having set the lead in aggressive honesty with *Les Valseuses*, had a tough act to follow – which, of course, he loved.

While waiting for the film to be released, he had quickly made another film for Marguerite Duras, with Bruno Nuytten again behind the camera. The story, *La Femme du Gange*, written by Duras who also directed, was described by her as two films, one the predictable and one the unpredictable. Depardieu was not in the lead, but was bred for his role, playing a sort of *plagiste*. The film ends, symbolically, with him standing rather deranged in front of the sea. It was not the sort of gritty realism for which he had developed an inclination, but it formed the second link in his enduring cinematic chain with Duras. And for him, an actor who seems to know intuitively where the camera is and where the frame line will cut him off in a shot, it was another test.

At about the same time he also had a strange and very short part as a young inventor in influential New Wave director Alain Resnais's political drama, *Stavisky*. (Resnais and Duras had made film history together with the powerful *Hiroshima Mon Amour*, his first feature, directed by him and scripted by Duras. The film is regarded by some critics as one of the three landmarks of world cinema along with *Citizen Kane* and *The Battleship Potemkin*, Resnais as one of cinema's greatest masters of style. A great innovator, most of whose films are charged with an enigmatic quality, he preferred to collaborate with well-known writers rather than write his own scripts. Resnais knew Depardieu through Duras.) The leading role of the seductive embezzler Alexandre Stavisky, a man who was the centre of a major corruption scandal in the 30s, was taken by Jean-Paul Belmondo who, it seems, didn't pull it off for some, judging by *Le Nouvel Observateur*'s headline above Jean-Louis Bory's review: '*Resnais, oui! Belmondo non!*' (A few years later Depardieu probably would have done the part.) Charles Boyer played the baron and Depardieu's stage colleague Michel Lonsdale the doctor.

Depardieu is in only one scene, as the impeccably neat, nameless young inventor trying to interest the older Stavisky in his revolutionary invention, a 'Matriscope' to tell in advance the sex of an unborn baby. His appearance is barely two minutes long, but in retrospect it can be seen as a symbolic meeting of the two generations of French cinema, face to face.

After *Stavisky*, Depardieu and Lonsdale were to cause considerable ripples in theatrical circles when they resumed ties with director Claude Régy for Austrian playwright Peter Handke's obscure and violent *La Chevauchée sur le Lac de Constance* (*Riding Over Lake Constance*) at L'Espace-Cardin. Nobody could understand why it was ever put on in Paris, but Depardieu got good reviews as critics noticed his ability to make savagery look real. He recalls the production as being an occasion with full audience participation.

'The only reason they came was to participate and give us things to eat – food like rotten tomatoes! The stage was covered with a whole meal at the end of each performance. We never had to go out for dinner after the show!'

When *Les Valseuses* came out in Paris and *Lac Constance* was being pelted nightly, Depardieu, by day, was shooting *Vincent, François, Paul et les Autres* with two idols of a previous generation, Yves Montand as Vincent, an industrialist, and Michel Piccoli as François, a doctor. The Paul of the title was Serge Reggiani and Depardieu was the most important of '*les autres*'. As Jean, he played a factory foreman.

Directed by Claude Sautet, the film is about a group of people and the effect on them when Vincent's estranged wife (Stéphane Audran) wants a legal separation. Depardieu, as the loyal Jean who helps Vincent sell the factory he owns, thus becoming jobless, is also an amateur boxer. It is a role perfectly suited to his abilities and the film was held up as an example when the boxing movie fad started in 1976 with *Rocky*.

Being particular about authenticity, Depardieu went into training for the role and at that very moment was summoned to Rome where Bernardo Bertolucci wanted to see him for a possible part in his film, *1900*. Depardieu nipped off to Italy with his agent Jean-Louis Livi of Artimedia to be interviewed. He arrived with a black eye, swollen jaw and split lip. Things hadn't gone as well as they might have back in rehearsals for *Vincent, François...*; but his battered look indubitably got him the role of Olmo, the peasant turned foot soldier in *1900*.

'*I'd searched worldwide to find two young actors who would immediately* ately give me the social feeling of one as a landowner and the other as a farmer,' recalls Bertolucci, 'Depardieu arrived looking like a popular epic poem. It was physically striking to see how he was, with his feet on the ground, like an oak tree. I could see his roots almost going into the earth.'

1900 would introduce Depardieu to the international market place but not for a couple of years. His first real breakthrough after *Les Valseuses* was his 1975 lead role in the BFI-trained Swiss director Claude Goretta's simple, touching *Pas Si Méchant Que Ça* (*Not As Wicked As All That*), with leading lady Marlène Jobert. He and Goretta had met fleetingly at a post-synch studio in Paris and in a matter of minutes had clicked so well that Goretta asked him to be in his next picture.

Depardieu was Pierre, a fresh-faced chap in dungarees who works for his father in his cabinet-making factory. Happily married and a loving father

Depardieu with Yves Montand, Michel Piccoli and Serge Reggiani as Jean, Vincent, François and Paul

Boxing in Vincent, François, Paul et les Autres, *1974*

to a couple of bouncing children (as, indeed he was offscreen), he's suddenly plunged into the full flood of responsibility and bankruptcy when his father dies. In order to pay his staff he decides to go out and rob a bank – but starts with a post office. During the hold-up, the nervous young robber meets Nelly (Jobert), a pretty post-mistress.

A neat portrait of the struggle of smalltown, smalltime people with frustrations they can't get to grips with, it was a sort of mini-*Bonnie and Clyde* with garlic. The film reflected the actor's amazing ability to be open and acutely human in the most ordinary surroundings. He let his eyes, on screen, be the windows to his soul, something he has continued throughout his career.

'For me the film corresponded to what I wanted to do, to show how easily one can become both responsible for and a victim of law, administration, everything about you,' Depardieu elaborates. 'I found the part of Pierre particularly fantastic for me because everything he is is linked to his childhood. Pierre *is* his little childhood upsets. If he was only a thug or was only blameless, the film would be less effective. But he is both responsible and a victim, which makes it simultaneously unsettling and pure.

'I kept thinking: would I do the same in his situation? I think your reactions to situations depend on imagination, on your choice of a solution which "transports" you most of all. You can never judge what you'd do when you're on the spot. Pierre feels himself compelled to practise hold-ups.'

Afterwards Jobert said of Depardieu that his work had 'the freshness of a child'. Few stars retain this freshness after one or two outings. Depardieu is somehow imbued with it.

The next Depardieu film to be released was the powerful *Sept Morts sur Ordonnance* (*Seven Deaths on Prescription*). This time he shared the lead – although they never acted together – with one of his heroes, Michel Piccoli. It was glowingly well received and Depardieu got his first César (French Oscar) nomination.

Based on a news item about an ambitious young surgeon who is driven to kill his wife (British-born, French-based actress Jane Birkin) and children before committing suicide in the same way as another surgeon (Piccoli) had done fifteen years before in the same provincial town, it has an almost Balzacian setting with its dark backdrop of the individual battling against the medical élite. Depardieu and Piccoli were hailed as the best actors of their respective generations by the prestigious *Les Nouvelles Littéraires*. Director Jacques Rouffio had made 'a hit by taking us into the air-conditioned nightmare of a medical clinic' (*Le Figaro*). Everybody loved it in particular for knocking the corrupt French medical system.

Depardieu also became the best of buddies with Birkin and her lover, singer Serge Gainsbourg. They were to join forces again within a couple of months in the late Gainsbourg's quirky *Je t'Aime, Moi Non Plus*. But first there was Barbet Schroeder's *Maîtresse*.

An excursion into eroticism and sado-masochism, *Maîtresse* is a bizarre parable. The dominatrix was played by Bulle Ogier, the costumes were by Karl Lagerfeld, the photography by the unparalleled Nestor Almendros. Depardieu got top billing for his role as the young unemployed provincial who becomes *la maîtresse*'s boyfriend and helps her beat the château set to heights of ecstasy. Michel Pilorgé played a young guest.

French reviewers fell over themselves to say things like 'Depardieu continues to astonish', while the American Catholic church condemned it as morally damnable due to baldly explicit sado-masochistic scenes. Generally the US critics roasted it. The cinematic bible of the United States, *Variety*, straddled the fence by remarking that it was 'rather like the footage of one of those Italian documentaries on global decadence'.

In Britain it was not submitted to the Board of Film Censors, and shown exclusively under club conditions at The Screen on The Hill with a provocative flier saying, 'To you, these will be the most incredible things ever to appear on the screen. To the Maîtresse, it's a job'. The real-life *maîtresse* it was based on, according to Schroeder, liked the film very much. Watching it now in the 1990s it doesn't merit the hellfire and brimstone it received when it was released. But it was decidedly a taste of what was to come in Depardieu's Shock-'Em-Rigid screen track record.

Maîtresse is about a cool lady who moonlights as boss bitch and, for a fee, does the terrible things men ask her to do to them in her mirrored basement apartment, while Dracula-like music pounds through a dozen tacky speakers. Her 'clients' in the film are real clients in masks and in two explicitly sadistic whipping scenes a real *maîtresse* did them as whipping is 'a very delicate thing', says Ogier. 'It starts fine and gets heavier.' The scene that most people complained about is the one where she takes a hammer and nails the penis of a client to a plank of wood.

Depardieu's part in it, as the brutal and tender Olivier, was hardly less insalubrious, with various scenes of spanking, oral sex with a bonded masochist, urinating on clients and, as he was to do with *déjà-vu* familiarity in Bertrand Blier's recent *Merci La Vie* years later, rectal finger-probing. At the time Schroeder told *Film Comment*, the magazine that was to cause Depardieu's American crash in 1991, that there were few actors, however experienced, to whom you could say: ' "Now, she'll take you into the other room and give you some money and ask you to pee in the face of someone you've never seen," and they would do it, as he did, on the first take.

'He helped me by not being scared of the subject,' said Schroeder with uncertain relief, having spent the shoot surrounded by people who, deep down, were. According to convent-educated Ogier, who researched her role with three of Paris's (then) five *maîtresses* who ran specialised sex houses, neither she nor Depardieu had known such a world existed before they took on the job. Most of the crew were also novices to sado-masochism.

'He was extraordinary to work with,' continues Schroeder. 'He's like Marlon Brando and Michel Simon in one person. He has the immense, devastating humanity of Simon. When working, he is completely relaxed and completely tense at the same time. I couldn't get him to rehearse the day before shooting as I did with the rest of the cast. I had to follow his way, which was a challenge. He starts from zero every morning. You can

THE SCREEN ON THE HILL

British poster for Maître sse

In Maîtresse, *1976, with Bulle Ogier, in a pose some people might feel epitomises his attitude to life*

discuss a scene with him but not rehearse in advance.

'Every take is different and as good as the one before. I sometimes shot extra takes just for the pleasure of it. I was fascinated to see how many variations he could bring.'

A month after *Maîtresse* opened in Paris in February 1976, Depardieu was on screen again in a small but searing cameo, guesting as a fighting homosexual in the Gainsbourg/Birkin *Je t'Aime, Moi Non Plus*, a cult film which still packs the cinema with a new generation of filmgoers. In it the painfully thin, waiflike Birkin plays a snack-bar waitress who runs off with former real-life model Joe Dalessandro, here a bisexual trucker called Krass. Gainsbourg (whose daughter with Birkin, Charlotte Gainsbourg, now stars with Depardieu in *Merci La Vie*) wrote, directed and produced it, and also wrote the theme song, 'Je t'Aime', which he and Birkin sang together.

Depardieu was attracted to Gainsbourg because he was more or less the creator of cult movies in France. He was also as unconventional as Depardieu in his approach to his work. Depardieu was thrilled to be working in the movie and did it for nothing. In fact, his only credit is bottom-billing as the-man-with-no-name, who appears only a couple of times. With his brown hair briskly curled, he's first seen at the Saturday-night hop, sitting drinking a beer and fingering his crotch. Next as a gay young blade in white slacks, he sits, bursting with sexual potency, straddled across a white horse with a docked tail and attempts to pick up one of the beautiful young men before riding off into the sun over Les Alpilles. It's wonderfully inconsequential stuff, but once again he showed how he could pull off sexually confusing roles and get away with it brilliantly. Although the risks he has taken in playing such roles, as well as talking in such unhampered terms about his attitude to sex, have begun to have a kickback effect on his image, the riveting thing about Depardieu is that he comes in a huge, hulkingly male package, yet can convey the most delicate femininity or even vulnerable homosexuality on screen with the simplest glance from an eye, or *frisson* of a lip. In an interview years ago with an erstwhile American flesh mag called *Game*, when asked if he was bisexual, he replied that he had done everything.

'Look, we are all like animals, *non*? I prefer *les filles, les femmes* – women! – for the moment, but I don't know, maybe in fifteen years . . . *bof*!'

Of course, being the celebrity who is prepared – or stupid enough – to stick his neck out and say things like that means he has had to take the rap; but whatever he says he stands by. He's prepared to forget himself and risk everything.

'To be an actor, it's not sufficient to make gestures, to recite a text. You've got to irritate, to provoke, to disturb . . . You must see, feel, listen, live and go!'

To play a crotch-scratching homosexual at twenty-eight with, admittedly, twenty films under his belt but only three leads, was perhaps dicing with the dark sides of showbiz fate. But then the European attitude to on-screen sexuality and nudity is light years removed from the English-speaking world's acceptance – or unacceptance – of it. America is still quivering with shock over that shadowy glance of Richard Gere's penis in *American Gigolo*, made in 1980, and in Britain films like *Castaway* perpetuate the accepted norm that only women are okay for full-frontal nudity.

In French films, nudity is not an issue. People get into bed and out of baths with no clothes on whatever sex they are. Once, during a blitz of seeing Depardieu films, out of twenty-two films I observed him immortalised on celluloid fully in the buff in thirteen. One would have no difficulty recognising him nude in the dark. Most men would be more than content to be equally endowed.

If there's no hang-up about nudity in French cinema, where the body isn't necessarily used as a tingling examination of sensuality, nor is there one about it in Depardieu's mind either. He says he considers his body as 'just an envelope of flesh around me' that he's never been particularly at ease with – just another body.

'My biggest battle is my excessiveness. I will always be an actor who smokes French cigarettes, eats like crazy, drinks too much wine and rides a motorbike; and who doesn't worry about what he looks like.'

7

Making 1900

Elisabeth Depardieu has always said of her husband that he changes the colour of his character with each new role. He becomes what he has to be for the part and stays like that till the film finishes. She often forgets to whom she is married. With characters like Danton and Cyrano, it's probably quite amusing, but less funny if he doesn't leave his roles at the front door when he's working on something abrasive or traumatic. Throughout his patently 'driven' life he admits he has been profoundly affected by his roles.

'I cannot leave them behind,' he states, as though it would be mad to expect him to. 'In the theatre, yes, but in films, I can't understand how anybody can do that.

'I feel like a painter who works all the time on the same canvas until it is finished. Until then it follows me everywhere. I don't work. I live. I don't memorise my text. My work is emotion. All film acting has to come from feeling. Always! Acting isn't a job, it's a passion. When the passion starts dissipating and the motivation wears down, you shouldn't go on.

'There are people like Jack Nicholson, Dustin Hoffman or Bobby de Niro who have different techniques. But too much technique is dangerous. Look what happened to Dalí with his painting. And for all of us actors, the dangers are the same, because we risk a portion of ourselves in every role. Actors express those emotions which are too strong for everyday life. That's why it's so hard, utilising this particular sensitivity. It is a privileged but dangerous profession. The emotions are not false. They are always something one has lived.

'I cannot do that for more than five minutes at a time, but I still have to live the role full-time. I'm not the sort of person who can just step out of his part as if it were a suit. It's a permanent tension. My characters always live in me for the three-month shoot. You sleep badly, you lead an unnatural life, you eat too much. You're usually alone. The people around you aren't your family. I can never go to sleep sober in a hotel bed. I always end up drunk, sleeping on the sofa.

'Then,' he adds with a huge smile showing his perfect, square teeth, 'if you're playing a murderer, you never stop killing people in your head.' Refusing to be shut in the cramped, stereotyping world of the stars, he's never looked for safe or comfortable roles. 'I like using my work, my parts, to bring to life everything which would otherwise never have seen the light of day.'

His character, Gérard, in Italian director Marco (*Red Desert*) Ferreri's film about sex, *La Dernière Femme* (*The Last Woman*), would, possibly, without him never have seen the light. From Depardieu's point of view, a role to risk everything on and from his wife's a nightmare, *La Dernière Femme* is a complex, no-holds-barred study of virility in relation to woman and man's sexual insecurities, a sort of cathartic view of role reversal. Considered in Europe as iconoclastic rather than daring (or disgusting, as it was in London), Depardieu castrates himself with an electric carving-knife so that he can become both mother and father to his son. The castration is, of course, symbolic, or, as described in the National Film Theatre programme when it played there as part of a Depardieu festival, 'a sharp lesson for phallocrats'.

'What I wanted to tell,' said Ferreri, a former veterinary student who attacked the consumer society so viciously in *La Grande Bouffe*, 'is a story which reveals some of the things that are inside everybody but which they can't express.'

Gérard is an unemployed engineer, bigoted husband and father. He works in one of those industrial ghettos on the edge of Paris. Left by his wife who has decided to throw over her domestic chores in favour of a feminist commune, he struggles with the paternal-maternal demands of a thirteen-month-old son, Pierrot. At the time off-screen Depardieu's own son was four and little Julie was two. The moral filament of the film must have connected somewhere in his head. At the time he said it wasn't that he went searching for directors who were 'shocking' but that he felt he needed directors who had the audacity to show scenes that go all the way.

'If they risk going all the way with me, I will play out their fantasies,' he says in his typically enigmatic style, crossing his muscular arms over his chest, sitting in a haze of cigarette smoke. He inhales deeply before continuing. 'Papa [as he calls Ferreri] was prepared to risk all. He asked me if I was the timorous type. "Why? What for?" I asked and he said: "Because I need someone who cuts his own cock off." I happen to love the work of Ferreri – *La Grande Bouffe*, what a film! – so that was okay by me. He inspired me but I really wet myself making that film more than any other.'

Depardieu plays the film mostly naked with an uncompromising sexual freedom, fondling himself to what the BBC's lawyers refer to as a 'vertically self-sustaining member'. Although the act of sex is simulated, it's presented in *La Dernière Femme* in exactly the same way the shockable fear most – brazenly, boisterously and boldly. Presented by Depardieu – big, insolent, heavy, mocking the intellectuals and bad-mouthing the establishment – the film had ramifications that went deep into the fundamentals of French society. Depardieu, 'part-Hercules, part-child', as one French critic has called him, merely smiles his innocent smile and switches to the subject of weight, his weight, 'this poor body I drag about'. Because he felt that a 'thin man, totally naked, is an undignified sight', he put on several stone for *La Dernière Femme*, eating three vast meals a day, a devotion to duty that afterwards had to be worn away by arduous days on the health farm where, bored with a diet of boiled fish and mineral water, he quit early to return to real food and decent wine.

'It's not gluttony but anxiety that puts on the kilos. I weighed seventy-six kilos when I first came to Paris and I've been up to 116 kilos, lost some of it, put it on again. In *Police*, Pialat and I got depressed, so we ate and drank. Then I lost thirteen kilos for *Jean de Florette* and, after *Cyrano*, had to drop twenty before starting *Green Card*. I was having trouble tying my shoes.'

The hunky Depardieu's co-stars in *La Dernière Femme*, again were Michel Piccoli, and Nathalie Baye ('It was a dark and mordant film,' she comments, 'but I was out of work and Gérard very kindly got the part to help tide me over.'). The 'last woman' of the script is sumptuous Italian actress Ornella Muti, as Valérie, the doe-eyed factory crèche supervisor, who moves in with Gérard and his son. Their relationship, although sexually olympian, is uneasy from the start. Valérie is passive and resentful. She wants more – conversation, for a start. Gérard, an impetuous and anxiously virile male, is confused. His masculinity is crumbling. Valérie gradually takes over the boy. Other women scorn his forever nude, often tumescent

With Ornella Muti in La Dernière Femme, *1976, before he castrates himself*

offerings and as he feels his manhood removed, he finishes off the job himself. Little Pierrot (a remarkable child called David Biffani) hovers around, his large round baby eyes agog, as he watches their every move.

It is a troubling if inconclusive film. 'It was difficult and complicated to make,' concedes Depardieu. 'It is not easy to cut off your own penis, least of all while a child is watching. But it isn't a problem for me that I make films like that. They are films that represent the problems of the age we're living in. It was the idea of the film that counted. It communicated a message that needed to be heard. A man doesn't have to lose his identity because he lives without sex.'

In France, the film was passed without the censors' X-label but got one in Britain. While *Variety* found it a 'crackling consciousness-raising film', it was loathed by much of the British press. John Coleman of the *New Statesman* said: '*The Last Woman* takes a prolonged stare at the wobbling buttocks, hanging belly and often auto-animated genitalia of a chap called Gérard Depardieu ... Ferreri has seen *Last Tango* and learnt nothing.'

The debate about it lasted for months. Controversy over Depardieu, already quite fretful, was elevated to the excitable. Certainly in France he was undeniably a star and his audiences respected his choice of role as a personal affair. But he didn't stick around to field the missiles. When the film came out in Paris in April 1976 he had tuned back into the throb of film life and was away shooting in Amsterdam, again with Bruno Nuytten.

The film was *Barocco*, directed by André Techiné, and Nuytten's girl-friend, Isabelle Adjani, had the lead. Marie-France Pisier played a prostitute and Depardieu a chap called Samson, a retired boxer who is implicated in a sordid political plot. (When the film's poster came out headlining Depardieu, he demanded that it be changed to show Adjani's name on top.) A tricksy story of how love is stronger than death, Samson is killed early on in the film but resuscitated by Adjani's love before the end. Depardieu plays the part of the victim, and also that of his own murderer, in a brown wig, contact lenses and five o'clock stubble. Mrs Depardieu is reported as remembering her husband being quite dreadful to live with at the time, as he apparently tested the role out on her, putting her through his paces.

The French press went wild about the coupling of the hot Depardieu and the cool Adjani, the ultimate explosive duo, a billing to dream about. (They were to repeat this electricity a decade later, directed by former cameraman Nuytten, in *Camille Claudel*.) But *Barocco* didn't work as well as it should have at the box office and was not the highpoint of Depardieu's year. Nor was *Baxter, Vera Baxter*, an esoteric Marguerite Duras film he made 'for a bottle of good wine' while shooting *Barocco* and in which he spends the whole film sitting in a beach café on the Pacific talking to Delphine Seyric about the enigmatic Vera Baxter (Claudine Gabay).

The high point was to come with the release in Paris in September 1976 of Part One and then, in November, Part Two of *1900*. It had taken director Bernardo Bertolucci a year and a half to edit. Almost a lifetime had passed between the shooting and the final release.

Bertolucci, well-known for his extravagant, brilliantly elaborate approaches to subjects like sexual power in *Last Tango in Paris* and, on an epic plain, China's Qing Dynasty in *The Last Emperor*, had been wanting to make a huge and political film about Italy ever since he'd filmed Alberto Moravia's powerful novel *The Conformist*, about Italy during the years of fascism in the 1930s.

He chose the lengthy novel *1900*, which interweaves the personal vicissitudes of two families, one wealthy and land-owning, the other poor and tenant-farming, over a canvas of time from 1900 to 1970, swept by social changes, the rise of fascism and the dissolution of the traditional agricultural society of Northern Italy. His starry cast was headed by Burt Lancaster, Donald Sutherland, Sterling Hayden, Robert De Niro and Depardieu. Lancaster was the grandfather of the villa, Sutherland the vicious fascist foreman, Hayden a tenant farmer. De Niro, who had just won an Oscar for Best Supporting Actor in *Godfather Part II*, played Alfredo, the son of the noble family, Depardieu Olmo, the bastard-born, peasant revolutionary. Sharing the same birthday in 1900, they live in almost adjoining homes, but their lives are worlds apart.

'For me making *1900* was a dream,' utters Depardieu, almost overwhelmed with excitement. 'I was working for fifteen months with people that I'd dreamed of since I was a child in Châteauroux. Burt Lancaster – I had been obsessed with him since boyhood, my hero from *Alcatraz*. There he was with that strong back! And Sterling Hayden from Nicholas Ray's Western *Johnny Guitar*, Bertolucci, people my own age like Bob De Niro, my friend Donald [Sutherland], all with different languages mixed together, a whole world encapsulated on an enormous plateau with no frontier. That's what cinema should be – an encapsulated world of its own.'

Sutherland remembers this world with amusement every time he looks in a mirror. He and Depardieu, both staying at the same hotel in Parma, spent many evenings together. On one, Sutherland did a live re-enactment of his day's work for a visiting American who was tagging along with them.

'We were pretty drunk, on brandy, at the bar of the hotel,' recalls Sutherland. 'The American was drunk too. It was late, two in the morning. I was bemoaning that during filming I'd allowed myself to be seduced into running head first into a wooden telephone pole so that the camera could have an intercut of my cranium bursting a blood-filled rubber cap. It had, I felt, nearly concussed me. Gérard was consoling me. He thought it had.

'To describe dramatically the action for the American I ran head first towards an aluminium pillar holding up the lounge ceiling. I tripped and crashed into it with my head. It wasn't aluminium. It was a mirror – a shattered mirror. There I was turning around and around, trying to find where the blood was coming from.' It came from his ear which had been guillotined by a large shard of glass. Continues Sutherland: 'Gérard came racing across the room, lifted me off my feet and with one hand at the scruff of my neck, the other holding my ear, propelled me to the hospital, laid me on a gurney, ordered doctors into the room, covered my face with a dark green cloth and frightened them into sewing my ear together. They were students and male nurses, and didn't know anything about anaesthetics. In French, a language they didn't speak, Gérard said he would

Depardieu in 1900

hold me down. He held me down with the flat of his hand, and his immense strength and determination. I gave up, they sewed.'

Seventeen stitches later, Depardieu carried Sutherland back to the hotel, took him to his room, tucked him into bed, held his hand and told him everything would be alright.

'He was my mother and father and Florence Nightingale,' says Sutherland. 'I think I was about four. I loved him.'

1900 was made in Italian (most of the actors were dubbed) and Depardieu was playing the role closest to his heart, the simple peasant, pastoral, physical, tied to the earth but with a mind of his own. Even when he had to kill and dismember a pig he seemed to know what he was doing. Through some ten months of shooting on location near Parma they spent their days getting up at 6 am and filming till seven at night, and three times a week watching the 'dailies', usually in a small parish hall.

Bertolucci remembers his two young leading men as very different and reports that they clashed.

'Bob was completely American school of acting. He needs preparation to enter into shot. The director has to *beg* him to enter into shot. Gérard you just push into shot. He has such a natural acting talent he walks into shot like somebody who walks home.

'The differences in their professional relationship was very evident. They were a bit like their characters. Bob stayed in a villa in the countryside, like a landowner, and his [then] wife [actress Diahnne Abbott] came to visit him. Gérard stayed in a small hotel where Elisabeth and the children were. Superficially Bob and Gérard had conflicts but basically they were both on the same adventure.'

De Niro, says Depardieu, was head of his own 'gang', a completely different one from Depardieu's, intellectual rather than instinctive. Not a method actor, he sometimes finds it difficult to work with those who are. In one scene when De Niro had to weep and the tears wouldn't flow, 'all of a sudden he entered the scene, hit me and then snapped his fingers for the camera to roll. He started to cry. After filming he said, "I'm sorry, Gérard, but I need to hurt somebody I love in order to cry." "Listen, my boy," said I, "I don't want to shoot this scene fifty times if that's what it's going to take for you to cry".

'I was still young and very *sauvage*, very wild. I don't think I understood him properly. When the press asked me about him I'd just say "*merde*".' I used to be very unfair on him but now I see that he has a great gift' – and this from the man whom the press love to call France's Robert De

As peasant revolutionary with Robert De Niro in 1900, *1976*

Niro. 'He makes a real sacrifice, like an artist, obsessed with the details. I didn't understand how he could be so possessed by a character. But I was young... I'm on a different route but perhaps we'll end up in the same place.'

At the time De Niro was distracted, preparing for his next role in *Taxi Driver*, and possibly didn't enjoy having to shoot an unclad scene with Depardieu, when they share their sexual ecstasies.

'Maybe I'd like to work with him again but I don't think he'd like to work with me!' *Chacun à son monde*...

'Bertolucci,' he said about the man who swept him into a world he'd hovered on the edges of for so long, 'is somebody who isn't motivated by facile passing goals. He lives life to the full, right down where it's born and created, where something significant is bursting through. I see him more as a great poet, rather like Victor Hugo. He is one of those directors like Pasolini who have social and political relationships with art.'

At first planned as six episodes for television, in elaborating the scenario Bertolucci, with his younger brother Giuseppe, also a film director, and editor Franco Arcalli, began to feel that for political, social and narrative reasons it belonged on the large screen. The first version was seven and a half hours long cut down to five and a half and split into two manageable parts. It was given arthouse status in Britain.

'It's an extraordinary film, one never tires of it,' declares Depardieu, who seldom sees his own films and is bothered that distributor pressure meant cuts. 'So what if it's long? It's truly great cinema, a new cinematic language. It's a sort of *Les Misérables* of its time.'

For Depardieu it was the signal to move on to the international scene. It was also confirmation that it was possible to do serious historical and political work, and still be popular.

8

Glad Days and Mad Dogs

Depardieu often talks about a sense of family that surrounds the cinema for him, about how filming is like playing cops and robbers with a bunch of schoolmates, having a great adventure as a close group of friends.

He seems to divide up his acting friends into the *copains de classe*, like Patrick Dewaere and Pierre Richard, and the father figures, like Jean Carmet, Michel Piccoli, Yves Montand. Within this extended family he feels the security he lacked in his rackety childhood and gleans the feedback constantly requried to keep the engines powered.

'Working with friends is most important to me,' he says, talking fluently and fast about one of his favourite topics. 'I need support, I need understanding. I'm interested in partnerships, in knowing each other deeply, working with trust and being able to relax and do good work. And staying friends through the bad times.'

Depardieu can slew from melancholy to tantrum within a flash, yet he always seems to end up on good terms with those he's working with. His flare-ups with director Maurice Pialat are no secret. For years they wouldn't speak to each other. Their most colourful exchange was an occasion when Depardieu described him as 'a lyrical toad'. The distinguished Pialat snapped back, saying the actor was 'a tank with a motorbike engine inside'. But that's long forgotten or, at least, forgiven: they have since made three films together, *Loulou*, *Police* and *Sous le Soleil de Satan*.

Like the songs of Georges Brassens that celebrate *'les copains d'abord'*, the 'pals above all' feeling, buddy-buddy friendship among men is probably prized on screen in France more than any other form of relationship.

'Among the people I work with, we have the same feel, the same smell – *parfum* – and because we all know each other so well we dare to do more. It's like a love affair – with epic battles, *bien sûr*!

'The precise art of acting interests me far less than the act of putting together an idea that will mean some form of communication. I love the smell of a new script. The script is something you make together as a group. Acting is like the dessert after the meal. The rest is the meal. That's why I like to work with the same people again and again.'

People like Pialat, Veber, Blier, Berri, Livi are on his small tested network of very close friends, most of whom, when he's in town, he telephones daily – particularly Jean-Louis Livi, his first agent, now his adviser and producer.

'When I first met Jean-Louis in those early days in Paris I felt as though I'd at last found a *copain de classe*, ready for some fun.' In his missive to Livi in *Lettres Volées*, he writes how between school and *le grand tourbillon de la vie* (the whirlpool of life), as Blier calls it, he never had any intermediate stages with a guide or an older woman to help launch him into the world knowing the rules of the game. He regrets not having had the comradeship of a real childhood, but is grateful that the acting profession has somehow allowed him to become a bit of a child working within this family of pals. Ideally, he would like to work 'in the style of the gypsies', with lots of people getting together, all a big family, moving around, having an adventure, telling the story.

For a man who tends to mix reel life with real life and who says he always chooses characters who represent the society he lives in, complete involvement came easily. In 1976 he formed a company, MAB-Films, to get further involved in and acting as co-producer on friends' projects.

'I did it not for business purposes or to dodge tax but to make more personal films. It is also a way not to crush a film under a star budget. I want to make films that are difficult, that others might hesitate to make.'

It was then that he moved the family to a base outside Paris, to an old three-level house in the winding village of Bougival. About fifteen miles due west of the city, set on a bend where the Seine swells, greening the Ile-de-France, as the region surrounding Paris is known, it's on the road to Versailles where the beauty is striking but simple. Discovered some time ago by the Impressionists, Bougival is one of those prosperous rural areas outside Paris where, in the nineteenth century, people went on Sunday to stroll among the wheatfields, to watch the *péniches* chug by and to listen to the larks sing. Sisley and Monet painted the Seine at Bougival, Pissaro the wash-house. Turgenev had a *dacha* there, where Maupassant, Saint-Saëns and Fauré visited him on Sundays. More recently, Bougival has been discovered by other French icons like Johnny Hallyday and Jean-Michel Jarre.

The house Depardieu bought on the hill above the river was 300 years old, and had a garden for Guillaume and Julie to grow up in, space for an orchard, a cellar for their wine. It was not a move towards a star's reclusive lifestyle but, at last, an anchor for the drifting emotions of a country boy who needed to be grounded in the soil.

'I had to leave Paris. I said to myself: "Listen, you're a peasant, Gérard. You're closer to the countryside than the city." And now the city is just a motorbike ride away.'

Thoroughly rooted, he dived into work to pay for his empire-building at a time when the crisis-ridden French film industry had forced many actors to take deferments or cuts, and even Depardieu, the top new name of the time, was reported to be broke – 'I have no idea of money.' He had no alternative but to get on and shoot back-to-back movies. At this stage in his career it is not clear whether he *was* working essentially for the money or for a workaholic's buzz, but back-to-back movie-making clashes with his saying that he didn't want to have a career 'like a civil servant' making film after film; the signs are that it was for the money.

'At the moment I only have my house and my debts and taxes,' he said. 'But I'll never be happy with just success or just money. My joy in life doesn't depend on that. You have to take some risks as well! How could I refuse to work with Blier again or Ferreri or my friend Gérard [Zingg]? Under what pretext – resting? That would be crazy. I don't need to rest. Lack of work stifles me.'

In 1977–78, ten Depardieu films were released. On some of them he was co-producer as well as lead actor. Some slipped by quietly, some were striking hits. *René La Canne* was the first. A war comedy set in 1942 in Paris during the Occupation, Depardieu plays a babyfaced criminal who, when arrested, pretends he's mad and gets himself interned in the asylum, ending up on familiar territory trafficking US surplus supplies. Director Francis Girod admits that the role was written to fit Depardieu. His screen girlfriend, Dutch actress Sylvia Kristel, is to be found running a house of comely delights, and father figures Jean Carmet and Michel Piccoli (for the third time) co-star.

Gossip columns on both sides of the Channel immediately paired off

Trafficking surplus with Piccoli and Sylvia Kristel in René La Canne

Kristel and Depardieu, most notably the *Daily Mail*'s Nigel Dempster describing her as 'coy' and him as 'eccentric'. Both laugh noisily at the suggestion. Depardieu is known for always being courteous and caring towards his leading ladies. Kristel later told me in London, when she was promoting *Lady Chatterley's Lover*, that it suited everyone to let a little aroma of spice emanate from the set to titillate the public before the film opened. 'It would have happened anyway. The press will never forget that I was once *Emmanuelle*. I will always be seen in soft-focus in their eyes!'

Depardieu's next film was his fourth with Marguerite Duras, playing a taciturn truckdriver in *Le Camion* (*The Truck*). He describes it: 'She started talking about the film one morning at half-past eight while we were in her car, on our way somewhere. Unknown to me, shooting was to start at ten o'clock the same morning. She knew perfectly well I didn't have to read the screenplay. I feel very strong when I am with Marguerite. I can be completely open and at her disposal. The first time we met she said, "You scare me, you're just right for the part!"'

In the film, which soon gained a reputation with the critics as a great non-movie, he sits and stares while she talks and talks in the conditional tense about a female hitch-hiker who gets into a truck. The film was selected for the French film section of the Cannes festival of that year. 'To the film I bring my listening,' he says good-naturedly. 'No way can you *pretend* to be listening...'

The next month, her other 'talking picture', *Baxter, Vera Baxter*, was released while he was making *Dîtes-Lui que Je l'Aime* for Claude Miller. The film of Patricia Highsmith's novel, *This Sweet Sickness*, Depardieu plays David, an anti-hero role as a provincial factory accountant neurotically in love with Lise (Dominique Laffin) and loved by Juliette (Miou-Miou). David visits the French Alps each weekend apparently to see his parents but, as Juliette discovers, he is actually building a house for his childhood sweetheart, Lise, who is now married to somebody else. Older and more experienced than in their *Valseuses* days, Depardieu's and Miou-Miou's obvious flair for sensitive characterisation of people unable to deal with unrequited love, and hiding fathomless latent violence, is chillingly reflected against the beautiful Alpine scenery. Depardieu, in a mac and specs, proved again that he was somebody of today, someone who could be a factory worker, which had only really happened before with Jean Gabin and Raimu, who remained *folklorique* men of the earth to the end.

Blier chose Depardieu because of his nature, which he saw as 'dangerous, aggressive, capable of anything'; and Miller told French film critic Robert Chazal that he chose him because on the surface he appears sweet and benign but with a violence that simmers below the surface. His apparent simplicity hides mysterious depths. This violence, one of Depardieu's recurring subjects of discussion, is something he can get very caught out on at interviews, as he appears to condone it while condemning power.

Depardieu's first role as co-producer was in Gérard Zingg's first film *La Nuit, Tous les Chats sont Gris* (*At Night All Cats are Grey*). He'd known Zingg since the latter was assistant to Claude Régy and then Bertrand Blier, and it was a project Depardieu, Donald Sutherland and actress Laura Betti had discussed while shooting *1900*. Sutherland fell out through over-commitment (Robert Stephens stood in) but Betti co-starred. Depardieu plays a small-time pimp on the Côte d'Azur (more familiar territory) called Philibert, who is the invented hero of bedtime stories told to a young girl by her British uncle.

'I made it because it is a piece of entertainment fantasy, the complete opposite of the film with a message, halfway between *Alice in Wonderland* and *Jekyll and Hyde*,' says the actor. 'It was fun and I wanted to show that I could also be a creator, not just an actor.'

It was, however, a colossal box-office failure.

He rounded off 1977 on a high with a real *'copains d'abord'* movie, *Préparez Vos Mouchoirs* (*Get Out Your Handkerchiefs*, i.e. you can cry if you want to). With his two best accomplices from *Les Valseuses*, director Blier and actor Dewaere, the film was paradise. It had a big budget, a terrific script, loads of publicity, and the Americans enjoyed it enormously. It also reaffirmed that redoubtable Blier–Depardieu writer-actor double act that has (so far) survived four films, with more in prospect.

'When we all met on the first day of filming we felt we were starting off where we'd left the last shot in *Les Valseuses*,' recalls Depardieu. Carole Laure replaced Miou-Miou (who was committed elsewhere) making up a trio who, through the film, don't know what they're about or where they're going. The story concerns a husband who, when he finds his beloved wife sulking unhappily, hands her over to a stranger in a bar in an attempt to cheer her up.

'To some extent I tried to recapture the style of *Les Valseuses*,' comments Blier, 'but although the dialogue for Depardieu and Dewaere has got a lot of cheek in it, the situations are less aggressive and the comic side has been strengthened.'

The tear-jerking comedy won them all the Oscar for Best Foreign Film of 1979, bringing international recognition, clout and bankability. Yet, six weeks later the new French leading man, Depardieu, was to reappear on screen in an obscure Swiss peasant drama called *Violanta* from a story by Conrad F. Meyer, popping up in a tiny role playing a killer. It was almost like the bad old days again, but he was passing and they were friends.

Next was one of Depardieu's more quirky films, *Rêve de Singe* (*Bye Bye Monkey*). Made in New York, he plays a Manhattan museum cleaner called Gérard, who's in love with a chimpanzee. James Coco, Marcello Mastroianni and Mimsy Farmer co-star with a chimp called Bella, whom Depardieu ends up treating as a son. The first time they met, they took to each other like brothers. It was also the first taste, for him, of working far from home, away from Europe. With scratchy English in New York he clearly loathed the experience. He was carved up on 'The Stanley Siegel Show' for failing to cope with the questions in English, and confided to the French magazine *Première* that without his wife and children he felt 'like a lion in a cage'. He never wanted again to find himself alone in a hotel room. But as his fame grew he was to find himself increasingly living in hotels; his wife even wrote a song 'Chambres d'Hôtel' for him to sing on the album he made a few years later. *Rêve de Singe* meanwhile got the 1978 Jury Prize at Cannes.

71

Another of life's great journeys, with Patrick Dewaere in Préparez Vos Mouchoirs, *1978*

At the same festival another Depardieu film, Peter Handke's *Die Links-händige Frau* (*The Left-Handed Woman*) was entered, representing Germany. Depardieu is merely listed as 'the man in the T-shirt' and his old stage partner half-English, half-French Michel Lonsdale co-stars. Perhaps becoming wary of so often being the saving grace of a film ('calming a choppy film down', said Truffaut), he took refuge in the stage again and went into rehearsal for Claude Régy in Handke's *Les Gens Déraisonnables sont en voie de Disparition* (*Unreasonable People Are on their Way Out*).

72

It was staged at a suburban theatre in Nanterre, outside Paris, and done for a basic wage.

'The theatre brings out a certain sort of discipline and humility. You can be an egomaniac one night and screw up the next,' he interjects, almost as an excuse for rushing back to the stage whenever he can.

On the first few nights, members of the Nanterre audience heckled the cast until, theatre legend goes, Depardieu, with his viking head and rough-hewn frame, stepped to the front of the stage and told them to be quiet or leave. The play completed its run to full houses of attentive audiences and transferred to the TNP at Villeurbanne in Lyons. One night after a performance, as he was leaving the theatre alone, a man attacked him.

The popular version of this story is that the two of them had been drinking in a bar, and the man wanted Depardieu to go with him and pick up some tarts, a suggestion the actor refused, whereupon the man set his German shepherd on him. The actual story appears to be that at two o'clock in the morning, while Depardieu was walking down an alley back to his digs, quietly reciting a speech, an unknown man stopped his van and set his dog on him. He was bitten all over, on his wrists, legs and body. There are scars still at his throat and snaking up his arms among the blue tattooes.

'You can't do anything about a dog trained to attack a man,' he says. 'It encircles you. It is not like a face-to-face confrontation with a knife. The best thing you can do is to stand still. It is very easy to be devoured by a dog.'

He spent five days in hospital, which set off a long, cascading depression that almost developed into a nervous breakdown. The incident obsessed him. He was shocked by the ferocity of it. It seemed somehow to underscore the real-life potential of so much of the characterisation he'd portrayed on screen. His preoccupation with the event led him to the analyst's couch. He had several sessions with the legendary French psychoanalyst, Jacques Lacan, and has continued with psychoanalysis on and off for years.

'I went into analysis as one would go to a dentist for a toothache. To cure it. It hurts if there's a pain in your soul. I truly recommend psychoanalysis to those who worry or feel uneasy in their skin. And afterwards you listen to others with generosity because you've said so much yourself. I didn't realise how much I needed to talk.'

The tenth film of Depardieu's frantic two-year spree was a biting comedy called *Le Sucre* (*The Sugar Swindle*). It won him a César nomination

Overcoming his fear of dogs in Les Chiens, *1979*

and gave him a first chance to play an aristocrat. As Viscount Renaud d'Homecourt de la Vibraye, he is a classy crook during the 1974 French sugar-shortage crisis. He laughed it off as being another 'hoodlum role', playing the baddy to Jean Carmet's goody. Michel Piccoli also stars and it was helmed by *Seven Deaths*' director, Jacques Ruffio. Certainly the film gave him a degree of security after the trauma of the dog.

The strangest thing of all about the dog case was that shortly after it happened, a new young director, Alain Jessua from Lyons, asked him to be in his political thriller *Les Chiens* (*The Dogs*), the story of a fascist Alsatian dog-trainer in a futuristic society who menaces and terrorises the local community with his dogs. Jessua didn't know that Depardieu had been attacked.

Depardieu reluctantly took the job, partly to conquer this new fear of dogs. For a month he worked in a protective canvas suit with trainer André Noël and his dogs. When he is 'killed', his (screen) Alsatian bitch was apparently so upset that she lay down by the prone actor and licked him until the take was over.

9

Not the Only Rhino at the Waterhole

Depardieu might have made a lot of films but he feels he has not made enough. His reasoning is that film is a means of communication and should convey a social message. There is no end to the number of social messages that can be captured within the framework of a script and, having an almost pathological desire to work, it suits him to make a lot of films. He doesn't take a job thinking it will please the public or do well at the box office. He takes it because it interests him.

'I can't stand boredom,' he says in response to critics who chastise him for not being choosier about his roles, admitting that his body of work is uneven and conceding 'there's a lot of crap, many failures'.

But the real reason is, of course, that for Depardieu, acting is an obsession. God knows what he'd do if he wasn't doing it. Once he tried, with Elisabeth, to write a script of his own. It was called *La Route* (*The Road*) and the social message was based on his own life. But it didn't come easily and he slid back into acting, when Maurice Pialat, one of the greatest of French realists with a sometimes awesomely bleak view of life, offered him *Loulou*. A peach of a role for Depardieu, *Loulou* had a rampantly virile social message about a culture clash across French social barriers. It was considered so explicit that it transcended the erotic.

Pialat and his leading man had had a chequered relationship in the past but Depardieu thought the story was so strong that it would be a waste of time to keep on fighting with Pialat. 'I think it is worth starting with an argument if it ends up nicely,' says Depardieu after the experience, where ricocheting tempers reached tornado proportions. 'I was a bit pretentious at the time and he was paranoid,' he adds, shifting around in his chair with a little giggle of perversity. Depardieu couldn't give a good-natured damn. Pialat, who has been described as hard to work with, was more cautious.

'Once we adapted ourselves to each other, we got on very well. I never had any doubts about his talents. As with other actors of his generation, he's offered films which are beneath his real value.'

Pialat describes the film as a rather ordinary story about a woman, Nelly (Isabelle Huppert), from a well-to-do social background who earns a good living in advertising. She's been living comfortably with a man in advertising but is beginning to become bored with him. One night in a disco she meets the leather-jacketed, smalltime hoodlum and stud Loulou (slang for 'slob' or 'darling'), irresistible to women and allergic to employment. She ends up keeping and living with him in rented rooms in a sleazy district of Paris filled with tawdry bars and pokey hotels.

'What's he got?' her spurned man grumbles.

'He never stops,' Nelly replies.

What follows is the tale of their curious and carnal love affair which got the two actors branded as the most anarchically sexual pair on screen. In six years, since their brief coupling in *Les Valseuses*, they had developed dangerously evocative screen personae. Depardieu, says Pialat, was the immediate choice for the part of Loulou. Sylvia Kristel refused the part of Nelly because it 'went against the brand image of herself she had obtained with *Emmanuelle*'. Isabelle Adjani and Miou-Miou were unavailable and just as Pialat was starting to worry he met Isabelle Huppert, whom he didn't know but liked.

'Their temperaments,' says Pialat, 'are as different as the characters they play, and yet as similar, too. Isabelle is a "secret" actress, reticent yet very active. Depardieu is very positive, so good you don't realise how much he puts into his roles.

'Sometimes I made him suffer, shut him up in oppressive scenes, in tiny settings, whereas he loves plenty of space. But something very vigorous came out of it, a Depardieu rather like a caged animal.'

The French didn't like *Loulou* much. It shocked them, even though since the early 70s there had been an alarming growth in the number of cinemas in France showing only pornography (which *Loulou* is not) and the industry was making more than a hundred porn films a year, about half the country's annual output. It did, however, please the critics and received a Best Film nomination at the 1981 Césars. (So did Depardieu's *Le Dernier*

Crossing social barriers in Loulou, *1980, with Isabelle Huppert*

Métro (*The Last Metro*) and *Mon Oncle d'Amérique* (*My American Uncle*).)

The Americans considered *Loulou* a typically modern, erotic French film and in Britain its explicitness was commented on: 'Isabelle and Gérard are always in bed, sex being the French equivalent of jogging,' Peter Ackroyd said in *The Spectator*. It did, however, have the courage to tackle the theme of class differences, usually as much avoided by French films as it has been the obsession of British ones. Depardieu, having delivered his social message as a sex-driven lout, then ambled off to the subdued grey of Northern European towns like Antwerp and Lille to make a comedy love story about a team of lady wrestlers.

Rosy La Bourrasque (*Hurricane Rosy*) was an Italian/French co-pro-duction directed by veteran Mario Monicelli. It takes place largely in a packed and smoky turn-of-century sports palace in Lille, one of the last strongholds of a sport threatened with extinction. The film tells of stormy affairs between a French-Canadian boxer on the skids (Depardieu) and a statuesque female wrestler known as Hurricane Rosy (a Brooklyn stuntwoman called Faith Minton). On set they called it 'broken bones and broken hearts'. It was also called 'Waiting for Depardieu', as they had to wait eighteen months for him to be free to film.

'This was an astonishing film,' he recalls of his individualistic hero role, 'and it was a strange experience for me because I was acting with this American girl, who is 1m 90 [about 6' 4"], and a whole team of wrestlers. Some of them were real women wrestlers with names like Hellcat Haggerty and Lola Garcia who unhesitatingly did arm locks, bear hugs and multiple varieties of the scissor move. I'm usually considered to be strong and hefty but I was the smallest among them. We were elephants in a china shop of emotions.'

For Depardieu it was a bit of a childhood dream come true as he had to do various acrobatic stunts and a few rounds in the ring with a former European champion Roland Bock, which resulted in a black eye. Then, while they were still shooting, the Oscars were announced. Another dream was about to come true for Blier's '*Valseuses II*'; *Préparez Vos Mouchoirs* won the Best Foreign Film section. This timely triumph came as Blier and Depardieu were about to tackle their third and blacker-than-pitch bite at the fabric of French society. Blier couldn't wait to use Depardieu again and this time moulded him with absurd lunacy in a virulent assault on the criminal system called *Buffet Froid*, set almost entirely in a soulless, nocturnal Paris of apartment blocks and Métro stations.

Depardieu plays a yob called Alphonse Tram. Like Depardieu, Alphonse always carries a knife in his pocket, something he uses to fiddle away unconsciously at things with. (During filming the actor would take his flick-knife home and Elisabeth would hear him clicking it in bed at night.) When his lost knife is found in a dying traveller on the Métro, Alphonse is suspected. But then, in Blier's alluring black comedy, nobody is wholly innocent and Alphonse becomes caught up with an assassin (Jean Carmet) and a police inspector (played by Blier senior, the now late Bernard). One has assassinated Alphonse's wife, the other is his new neighbour. (Carole Bouquet, his wife in *Trop Belle Pour Toi*, plays the young woman in the car.)

Lulled by an inspired screenplay based on an idea germinated by something Depardieu had said during the making of *Les Valseuses*, he once again dynamically sends himself up in this film that became a cult picture. Although made before it was safe to give prizes to the brilliantly outrageous, in France almost as many people saw it as they did *Danton*, his hugely successful classical drama about the Revolution.

Buffet Froid *with Jean Carmet, 1979*

'With Blier each film takes you further along the same track,' says Depardieu. 'His personal touch is to be scandalous, to walk on the wild side. He writes his films himself and shoots them in rapid "French style" on a small budget and with a feeling of urgency. It's like a thunder clap.'

Depardieu was to go almost all the way in their next collaboration, *Tenue de Soirée* (*Evening Dress*) and, some think, even further, beyond the limits, with *Merci La Vie* (*Thank You Life*); but what people think of the characters he chooses to depict on screen doesn't bother him. When *Merci La Vie* was first screened in Paris people actually went so far as to threaten him. As usual, Depardieu is laconic about it. They confuse the man and the role, he says in a gossamer-edged voice – an easy mistake to make, considering the closeness he brings to it.

'I have tried to preserve a kind of continuity of characters. I used almost to look for negative ones because I find it exciting to breathe life, emotion and ambiguity into them. The hardest roles are always the ordinary, everyday characters and how to make them interesting. The wimp is the worst.'

The only real wimp he's ever played was in Alain Resnais's *Mon Oncle d'Amérique*. Resnais, who'd liked him in *Stavisky*, picked him because of his melodic voice which he'd already used to double for the character of

David in his film *Providence*. (There's also a story that Depardieu was chosen to be in the film because he brings to the set a sense of *joie de vivre* and this film was going to be an incredibly tense shoot.) A fascinatingly assembled but basically bleak dissection of human life, the 'American Uncle' is the piece of good luck, which may just be round the corner (but probably isn't). It is based on the principles of French biologist, Henri Laborit, explaining the lives and careers, in terms of animal behaviour, of three very different characters who will all impinge upon one another as the action proceeds: René Raguneau, the farmer's son, Jean, the provincial bourgeois, and Janine, the metal worker's daughter born in Paris. Resnais describes his film as a process of 'weaving different threads into a carpet'.

As René Ragueneau, Catholic peasant, wimp *exceptionel*, Depardieu is the innocent from Anjou who breaks with family tradition to become a manager in a textile factory on the brink of bankruptcy. He also suffers stress, gets a stomach ulcer and is unable to show his feelings as he grovels his way from country boy to manager. His only passion in life is to go and see Jean Gabin movies.

Depardieu has neatly cut hair in the film, a suit and tie, and sweats his way through a period of crisis. Unlike anything he had done before, his performance is so tightly controlled you can hear the stress of his springs straining to unwind as Ragueneau emotionally implodes. The role was not, however, as effortless as usual. He never knew what was happening, did not find the role an interesting one and didn't like the film while making it.

'I don't think I'll ever play that sort of role again, of a man who was breaking down from the inside – like a nervous breakdown but not expressing anything. That's what ordinary roles of everyday people are about! I think the real reason why Resnais cast me was because he linked me in his mind with Jean Gabin, man-of-the-earth, everyman hero. Only later, when I saw the film, did I see the intricate interplay of the characters. Resnais deals with the subject of inhibition but it's difficult to sum up the story in a few words. It is very original.' And very *auteur*-New Wave style, rather than *auteur*-Depardieu style (when a team gets together and all become *auteurs*).

While shooting Resnais's film, a very silly Italian comedy of his was released. Made at Rome's Cinecitta in 1978 for Luigi Comencini, it was called *Le Grand Embouteillage* (*The Great Traffic Jam*). It starred Miou-Miou and Patrick Dewaere, and just about every post-war Italian cinema character, and reel by reel turned into a sort of chaos powered by the

Mon Oncle d'Amérique, *with Roger Pierre, 1980*

exhaust fumes of the *autostrada*. If Depardieu was feeling at all stressed about keeping his emotional lid on for *auteurs*, he must have felt relieved to know there were uncomplicated buddy-buddy movies around where one could still behave like a kid, fooling around with chums in the hoodlum vein.

Mon Oncle d'Amérique, whether he liked it or not, stood him in good stead. On the chart of his box-office successes it is in seventeenth place. Released in May 1980, it took the Special Jury Prize at the 1980 Cannes Film Festival, was nominated for Best Foreign Film at the 1981 Oscars and Best Film at the 1981 Césars. In a way the film also marked a new departure for Depardieu, from the manically frenzied parts of the 70s to more reflective, cerebral roles. As a new decade started he was to become cannier, more '*intello*', a word he despises but which describes a path of natural progression after all the rough and tumble he'd been through. It was time for a change.

By 1980, when *Mon Oncle d'Amérique* was released, he had made thirty-five films. A few had been exported and some had made their mark at the international festivals. *Préparez Vos Mouchoirs* had won the 1979 Best Foreign Film Oscar in America, and in 1978 and 1979 respectively *Rêve de Singe* and *Mon Oncle* had taken the Grand Prix Spécial du Jury at the Cannes festival.

He was to become a regular showbiz favourite at Cannes all through the 80s while promoting his films and one of the few European actors who genuinely generated interest in the international press; until then it had been Gérard Who? for audiences beyond European shores. Moving in the 80s to the media spotlight on the interview circuit, he arrived laden with an endless supply of gems for journalists, ranging from the naively boisterous and rude (about directors) to epic all-night benders fuelled by wine and the sense of sheer devilry the French permit their *monstres sacres* to have. Quickly he made a place for himself in the off-screen publicity machine, giving as good as he got to press and public.

While one minute he will be quipping that the film festival at Cannes is more vulgar than an event for local hairdressers (not entirely untrue) or telling a breath-takingly dirty joke without batting an eyelid, the next he will be lolloping out of one of the great banquets thrown at Cannes genuinely concerned about who is paying for it all.

'I love Cannes and I love festivals. I'm just a peasant, selling my wares, and Cannes is a market where you have meetings to sell your films. I hate leaving a film. It becomes part of me. I want, like a painter, to keep going back and touch it up and add a little more.'

It's a different way of thinking from most stars who can't wait to cut out after they've done their contractually-binding 'x' hours of publicity there. But then Depardieu isn't like most stars. For a start he's unpredictable: you never know on or off screen what he's going to do next. And secondly he chooses to be a star only when he wants to.

'I've never wanted to be a rhinoceros in the jungle, shoving everyone out of the way and drinking alone at the watering hole. I like to drink with everybody else.'

In the jungle at Cannes, he most certainly does.

10

The New Decade

As with everything, when Depardieu decides to do something he simply dives in. To be around him when he does is to be sucked into the tornado.

In 1980 he decided he wanted to sing. He disappeared into the hills above the Côte d'Azur to a villa-cum-recording studio near Cannes to recorded his first album. It took two days.

'This wasn't a sudden whim,' he says. 'I sing just as seriously as I act. I think an actor is quite justified in enriching his career by playing in the theatre and attempting to sing. I sing for pleasure, not for money. I won't kiss the radio programmers' boots to get them to play my record. Without the money I earn from the cinema I wouldn't be able to make records.'

Called *J'ai Tant Rêvé* (*I've Dreamed So Much*), it is a charming album of old-fashioned French songs in the Yves Montand style with Brassens overtones, a tribute to traditional *chansonnerie*. It is relaxed and amusingly understated, the singing boulevardier at ease in his skin. The songs, he rather chauvinistically explains, were written by his wife who actually wanted to sing them herself but he thought they suited him so well that he took them over.

Elisabeth, who has made a name for herself as a singer and was seen singing in *Jean de Florette* as Jean's wife, is credited on the cover. The album, with its stylised 60s cover of Depardieu's face in black and white on the front, stamped with '*ils ont dit moteur*', and the back of his head and '*coupez*' on the other side, has ten songs which certainly reflect his 'brute-who-can-cry' side. There are the traditional songs about ladies with pretty umbrellas to protect them from drizzle and tempests of sadness; there are also a couple of irreverent ones about being alone with body odour, graphically called 'I stink' ('Je pue'), and having a mad wife ('Ma femme est folle'), and several based on the acting industry. 'Le Cinéma d'Papa' with its honky-tonk piano and unsubdued vitality is a national favourite and named after Claude Berri's wonderful film, *Le Cinéma de Papa*.

The album came out as the new decade started, almost as a flag to indicate that things were moving in the Depardieu camp, changing and expanding, but in a tightly controlled manner. Over the next ten years Depardieu's career was to show him as a mercurial actor who could compete in the international marketplace with casual ease. Whether seen as a slow-witted slob or irresistible innocent, for there have always been two camps on the Depardieu patch, he became, after Catherine Deneuve, the French star audiences in the anglophone world knew best.

The link is appropriate; Depardieu had always been an adoring fan of Deneuve. She was five years older than he, came from a drama-steeped family and had been making films since 1959, when he was still a schoolboy. As he saw it, her unique allure made her 'a distinguished *bourgeoise* idol', while he was 'a peasant's son with strong hands'. Together, in Depardieu's first film for the late François Truffaut, *Le Dernier Métro* (*The Last Metro*), they were to make what Depardieu describes as 'almost a social conquest'. They are now old friends.

'I have a friendship with Gérard that's free of ulterior motives, so there's no simpering, no attempts to seduce him,' says Deneuve. 'Since he knows that I really am a woman with a complicated life and children, he knows I am not entirely this clear, direct person that I am on screen. Like a lot of actors, he's very feminine and his feminine side reacts to my masculine side.'

Depardieu had also always been in awe of Truffaut's universally acknow-ledged brilliance. Truffaut, for his part, knew Depardieu from the films of Blier. Jeanne Moreau introduced the two men.

'When I see an actor who might have a special sort of "mythology" for a part, or hear a piece of music that would illustrate it, the action takes off,' he told me in London in 1980 when promoting his book *The Films in My Life*. 'I saw Depardieu, and both myth and music happened! He was comparatively unknown and still hungry to learn. He still had a lot to learn but proved an excellent student.'

For Depardieu to get both Truffaut and Deneuve plus a marvellous

César-winning and Oscar-nominated in Le Dernier Métro, *1980, with Catherine Deneuve*

script in *The Last Métro* was for him one of life's great feasts. On top of that, to have Catherine Deneuve's character Marion comment on his stage performance in the film as being '*un peu dans le genre de Jean Gabin*' ('a little in the style of Jean Gabin') must have been like sipping at the finest of liqueurs. He said that the film finally showed him what he could do with acting.

Truffaut was inspired by actor Jean Marais's autobiography as well as other documents by and about theatre people during the Occupation. He said he wanted to fulfil three of his dreams: to take the camera backstage at a theatre; to evoke the climate of the German Occupation of France; and to give Deneuve the role of a responsible woman. 'A bit of the *Jules et Jim* with two men and one woman, who is in charge,' he added. The film, which he described as one of 'love and adventure', started shooting in Paris on 28 January 1980. The 'last *métro*' of the title is the last tube home within the 11 pm Nazi curfew. The film is set in Paris in 1942, when many French citizens bowed to pressure and collaborated to some degree with the Nazis. It marginalises the events of the Second World War and settles on the situation of a respected German-Jewish stage director (Heinz Bennent) who has to hide in the cellars of his prestigious Théâtre Montmartre, while his beautiful and sophisticated (non-Jewish) actress wife Marion (Deneuve) runs the theatre. She engages a new actor, Bernard Granger (a boyish Depardieu, using for the first time a voice that rises, *Cyrano*-like, almost naturally into couplets), a compulsive womaniser and secret member of the Resistance, who becomes their leading man. More interested in Marion than her Jewish husband's play, ultimately he becomes her lover. The scene, in this perfectly controlled film, when they finally acknowledge their confused passion for each other, without so much as a button being undone, still shoots down in erotic flames just about every screen love scene you care to recall.

'Because the film takes place during the Occupation, Truffaut wanted us actors to live all-day long in a clandestine atmosphere similar to the one that existed then,' Depardieu remembers. 'It worked very well. Shut up in the theatre the whole day, dressed in 1942 fashion, we had the feeling we'd gone back in time and our acting gained in authenticity.'

Their authenticity and Truffaut's fascinating evocation of atmosphere was rewarded with ten Césars, a Best Foreign Film Oscar nomination and the Grand Prix of L'Académie Française. In Paris it ran for seven months and more than a million people saw it on first release at the cinema. It was named as the best movie of the 80s at the 1990 César ceremony. It also marked Depardieu's first César for Best Actor. (The second was in 1991 for *Cyrano de Bergerac*.) When he went on stage to receive the oblong golden trophy he simply said: '*Enfin*...!' 'At last!' By the time that happened, Depardieu and Deneuve had already moved on together to do another film, Claude Berri's *Je Vous Aime* (*I Love You*).

Berri, like Truffaut before him, saw his film actually hanging on Catherine Deneuve.

'I wanted to give her a very great sentimental role,' said director Berri, who had just finished producing Roman Polanski's *Tess*. 'I'm glad she accepted, otherwise my film wouldn't have been made, since my story was written with her in mind.'

The film is about the love-life of a respectable woman in her thirties called Alice over a period of fifteen years. Serge Gainsbourg, at one time her off-screen boyfriend, plays her first love. Depardieu, Jean-Louis Trintignant and Alain Souchon play the others. Depardieu is Love Number Two, the fiery roughneck Patrick.

'Alice finds in Patrick a more unpolished type of man whom she treats

Je Vous Aime – *both, says Deneuve to Depardieu and Jean-Louis Trintignant,*
1980

in Pygmalion style,' says Berri. 'He is a rock 'n' roll idol and she introduces
him to a world which is less artificial than the one he lives in. In a moment
of bliss, they decide to have a child together, but from the day the child
arrives she cannot stand the idea that the lover has become a father and
leaves him.'

The night I saw it, in the scene where Depardieu and Deneuve are
fighting and he yells at her, 'Why won't you sleep with me now?' and she
looks at him and says, 'Because I don't find you sexy any more', a wave
of murmuring disbelief went through the audience. Deneuve, at the time,
citing his role in *Je Vous Aime*, selected the film as being nearest to catching
the quintessential Depardieu. (Since then, *Green Card*, a film based loosely
on his early lifestyle, would have to supersede.) Gainsbourg wrote the
songs for *Je Vous Aime*, many of which he and Deneuve croon together,
and Depardieu makes his first official appearance as a singer/saxophonist
belting out two rock numbers. Ever enthusiastic, he explained that as actors
were more or less always frustrated, to sing and take risks on one's own
was a new and stimulating way to communicate.

The interchangeable acting/singing side of French actors was clearly a burgeoning sideline then. Michel Blanc had made a record, Alain Souchon, a singer, had only recently ventured into acting and Catherine Deneuve made a disc of her songs with Gainsbourg from the film. Depardieu went on the popular TV chat-show *Numéro Un* and, in a flat-top leather cap, sang songs from his new album. Like his friend, Johnny Hallyday, a singer who has dabbled in acting, he has a good line in variety, moving nimbly on his dramatic feet, winning the audience over with his cleft chin and café-society voice, unafraid of making a fool of himself.

Depardieu's singing abilities, however charming, have stood him in reasonably good stead but not proved to be infallible. Word on the grapevine has it that when the late director Jacques Demy was planning a film called *Chambre en Ville*, a light, musical film along the lines of his much earlier *Les Parapluies de Cherbourg* (*Umbrellas of Cherbourg*), he wanted Depardieu and Deneuve. The film was to be almost entirely sung and when the two stars refused to be dubbed, wanting to do their own singing, they were dropped from the project – or so the story goes. (The film was recast with Richard Berry and Dominique Sanda.)

In 1980, Depardieu interrupted his year of film-making with a summer break back in Châteauroux where, in July, he was invited to collect the keys of the town and be heralded as a citizen of honour. They started the month with a festival of his films. On either side of the main roads into town signboards were sunk in the earth saying '*Festival Gérard Depardieu 1–6 juillet*'. On the sixth they gave him the keys of the town and got him to open the Fête Foraine, the floral festival that was taking place in the new gardens of the Cordeliers in the middle of town, just on the edge of the park where he had roamed as a child and done business as a teenager. It was the triumphant return of the *enfant terrible*.

His parents were there, together with the press and everybody who knew him. His sister Catherine, who was working in the town's toy factory, was there with Alain, Hélène and Eric. Even Franck, who was doing his military service in Versailles, got time off to attend. Elisabeth and the children joined the family group. There was an enormous crowd. The main square was blocked with official cars and the Gold Stars drum majorettes poured through the streets. The town displayed its best ribbons and flowers for this reception and the (then) mayor Daniel Bernardet was in his most formal suit. 'Châteauroux is proud of you today,' he said to the town's most famous son.

Depardieu, also in his best suit, did a grand walkabout shaking hands, hugging old friends, posing for photos and holding babies in his arms. As he stood up to address the crowd, his voice quivering with emotion, he said: 'Life sometimes has strange quirks.' The crowd went wild with delight to have their own *voyou* back. When the time came for him to cut the symbolic cord and open the new gardens, he turned to his wife who was standing at the foot of the platform with Guillaume and Julie, and gestured to them to join him. The crowd went wild again. By the time he kissed Elisabeth and said, 'Without my wife I wouldn't be here today', they were nearly delirious.

Depardieu's mother, La Lilette, in her bold-print floral frock, shed tears of pent-up emotion as her son brandished the keys of Châteauroux. '*Je suis fière de lui!*' ('I'm proud of him') the headlines screamed above her tear-stained face. Afterwards there was the banquet, hosted by childhood friend Sophie Bardet and her husband Jean, a restaurateur *gastronomique* who'd come from their hotel in Tours to do the catering. Depardieu let the photographers take pictures, for the first time, of him with his family, of Le Dédé with a granddaughter on his knee, La Lilette with her hands on her grandson's shoulders. The prodigal son's return somehow seemed to put the record straight, simply and sweetly. It was the ultimate redemption for their hoodlum. Depardieu found it strange to be welcomed back to a town that had previously never liked him.

Down the road, at the Apollo Cinema, they were queuing for *Préparez Vos Mouchoirs* which was playing double bill with *Mon Oncle d'Amérique*. In the Salle Racine *Dîtes-Lui que Je l'Aime* was being screened. So were *Les Valseuses, 1900* and *Le Sucre*. Outside was a board bearing a picture of Gérard and Elisabeth, a mugshot and four publicity pictures from the films fluttered in the breeze. There hadn't been such a celebration in town since Châteauroux's other leading man, General Bertrand, *aide-de-camp* to Napoleon, came home after Waterloo.

Bolstered by the high of acceptance, Depardieu returned to Bougival and Paris, to the next film.

Farceur Claude Zidi, best known for his hit *Le Cop*, is a director who specialises in cop comedy *à la française*. Depardieu had always wanted to do a regular comic role. When friend and fellow romantic Zidi mentioned that he was making *Inspecteur la Bavure* (*Inspector Blunder*), there was no question of him not being in the film. He knew Zidi worked like greased lightning – or, as he put it, *un homme 'speedy'*. Zidi was another man in a hurry.

Depardieu plays Roger Morzini, 'Public Enemy No 1', very dark (through prosthetic plastic surgery), very '*gangster*'. He is being hotly pursued by a bungling policeman (the late, great Coluche) who is in turn harassed by a beautiful young journalist (Dominique Lavanant). Michel Pilorgé is also in it. Although full of farce and frantic action (like putting cars on the top of columns), the film keenly observes the world of police irregularities and was one of the box-office successes of the year. It was also Depardieu's first major success in a mainstream comedy. The scene where he holds up a 'sheltered employment' factory full of disabled people in wheelchairs who mow him down is one of his most hilarious screen moments. Given Depardieu's eye for human absurdity and 'I-have-to-tell-the-truth-the-way-I-see-it' approach, it showed that even a sacred cow like disability can feature in a comedy – with a little help from everyone's favourite *voyou*, of course.

11

Truffaut for Dessert

Depardieu hesitated about accepting Alain Corneau's offer of a role in *Le Choix des Armes* (*Choice of Weapons*) with Yves Montand and Catherine Deneuve. He was to play an escaped prisoner, Mickey, another *voyou*, and he felt that with *Dernier Métro* and *Oncle d'Amérique* he'd managed to kick the typecast heavy hood. Yet it had two of his favourite actors in it and he *was* going to make another Truffaut film, so after debating with his agent Livi, and suitably persuaded that although violent, the film stood against violence, he agreed to go ahead. Moreover, it was a *policier*, something not to be overlooked in France.

Le Choix des Armes opens early one morning with two men (Depardieu and Michel Galabru) making a prison break. At the same time, thirty miles away, a wealthy stud-owner (Montand) and his wife (Deneuve) get up to tend a sick mare. But Montand is actually a retired gangster, and Galabru a former colleague. When the two escapees have nowhere left to go, it is *chez* Montand that they head for a spiritual lead.

Lyrical and violent – even Deneuve gets killed – the film, with its payment of social debts, touched a strand of morality in the actor.

'The gangster character, Mickey, is terribly dark,' Depardieu told the magazine *Voir*. 'It was an image that frightened me. Some nights during filming I couldn't go home, other nights I'd return, but sleep with my clothes on.'

Deneuve remembers him having trouble with the film. 'When we were shooting there was a violent scene where he throws me against a wall. He couldn't do it. We did it a number of times and he was very pale. We weren't able really to shoot it until the next morning, something that normally never happens with him. When he did it, he really did do it. In fact, he hurt me. But the whole business of hurting a woman posed a problem for him.'

Whatever deep-seated anxieties that emerged, at a time when he was still doing regular sessions in analysis, Depardieu is pleased with the film. He liked director Corneau, with whom he would make *Fort Saganne* a couple of years later, and working in tandem with one of his heroes, Montand, for the first time since *Vincent, François, Paul et les Autres* was a bonus. The film was a showcase, anyway, for the older generation and the new one. (Montand has always thought Depardieu is one of the best actors in the world, so the admiration is mutual. 'He is the actor of the new generation. I don't mean one of them. He is *the* one,' he told *Time* magazine in their *One-Man New Wave* cover story in February 1984.)

With the esteemed *Choix des Armes* coming in the wake of *Inspecteur la Bavure* and *Le Dernier Métro*, the French public's love affair with Depardieu was finally sealed. Those who didn't like him because of his success or his ham-fisted lack of finesse had to admit he *could* act, everything from Duras's minimalistic or Resnais's elaborate esoterica to mass-market comedy, tender love stories and compelling lowlife villains. He'd never hamstrung himself with a signature style. He was a popular actor and an artist.

'I'm the perfect turncoat,' is how the actor describes his versatility. Says Corneau: 'He can skip from one film to another twenty-four hours later without missing a beat. Most actors wouldn't even consider it. It's a mystery to me how he does it.' For the Gérard Depardieu who lived his roles, it was time to show his public that he could do an absolutely straight love story – no electric carving knives, whips, guns, social imbalances or sadism.

It was on the evening of the 1981 Césars, after Depardieu had gone on stage at the Palais de Congrès to collect his award for *Le Dernier Métro*, that François Truffaut saw a new side to the actor.

'It was on that evening in March I had the chance to see, side by side, Gérard Depardieu and Fanny Ardant, and I immediately felt I had there the makings of an exciting screen-couple,' he wrote in the production notes of *La Femme d'à Côté* (*The Woman Next Door*). 'Two great presences – the man fair-haired and apparently simple but actually complicated, the woman brunette and apparently complicated but in reality as simple as an open book. The filming of *Le Dernier Métro* had been too strenuous, too time-consuming to leave me any opportunity to consider a new project – until I saw Depardieu and Ardant together at the Césars.'

He knew Ardant's acting from a TV drama series called 'Les Dames de la Côte' ('The Ladies from the Coast') which was transmitted two weeks before he started shooting *Le Dernier Métro*.

'She and Depardieu both had the qualities I most look for in my actors and actresses – vitality, courage, enthusiasm, humour, but also, on the other side of the scales, a sense of secrecy, a savage touch, above all something vibrant. From the moment we started filming I was given the confirmation that we had the right woman for our "woman next door" and the right man as the self-destructive lover.

'When I was shooting *Jules et Jim* in 1961 I had the feeling everyday that thanks to Jeanne Moreau and Oskar Werner, the film would be superior to the script. During *Femme d'à Côté*, thanks to Fanny and Gérard, I had the same impression again.'

Truffaut was a director who was fascinated by obsessive love. The love story here is one between Bernard and Mathilde who, seven years before, have had a tumultuous love affair that ended suddenly. The next time they meet they are both married to someone else, Bernard (an engineer) to Arlette, mother of his son, and Mathilde (a children's book illustrator) to Philippe, an older man. They meet when Philippe and Mathilde move into the house next door to Bernard and Arlette. Bernard appears to have found reasonable happiness with Arlette, and Mathilde seems to have found in Philippe the security she was searching for – yet when their eyes meet . . .

'When Fanny looked at me to say hello,' he told Truffaut after shooting the first scene in which the two ex-lovers meet again, 'she absolutely terrified me. I can see what kind of a film we're making here: a love story that will frighten people.'

Bernard, a suburban family man who goes to work at the oil refinery outside town, becomes obsessed with Mathilde again. He starts watching, his eyes dangerously dark, as her lights go on and off, monitoring her movements, charting her life as he battles with a severe bout of *amour fou*. In a single look, a single smile, he expresses the agony of a tortured heart. One evening his wife unknowingly invites them over to dinner. Bernard can hardly cope. He finally asks Mathilde to meet him. At first she is reluctant, then she goes. They start to meet regularly, their secret guarded by the manageress of the local country club who, years before, also had a wild but forbidden romance.

With Fanny Ardant, La Femme d'à Côté, *1981*

Making the film was by all accounts a pleasure. Depardieu and Ardant knew each other from making *Les Chiens* together a couple of years before. Truffaut and Ardant at the time were lovers – he is the father of the second of her three children – and he and Depardieu got along famously.

'Depardieu isn't an intellectual in the traditional sense,' he explained, 'but when he talks of a person, a feeling or a film, his precision is dazzling. I have never met an actor who can change expressions so quickly.' ('He can go, in a split second, from slipping a frog down the dress of a script girl to throwing himself at the bedside of his dying mother,' said *Le Monde* critic Jean-Michel Frodon.)

They were tentatively scheduled to make *Nez de Cuir* (*Nose of Leather*), a love story about a Don Juan who wears a mask because his face has been disfigured, but in 1984 Truffaut died of cancer. Depardieu was with Truffaut in Normandy when the director first noticed the tumour that killed him. Obviously devastated by the loss of a mentor, Depardieu has said that although he talked to him often by phone when he became ill, he was unable to go and see him in that state.

'He was the archdiplomat who kept them all together – Godard, Chabrol, Rohmer, Resnais,' he adds sadly. 'He directed the family.'

What Truffaut and Depardieu could have done together in *Nez de Cuir* is beyond speculation.

The subject of Depardieu and film mutilation and deformity is not one he shies away from. It is something he seems to act out on a recurring basis. He is decapitated in *Danton*, hanged and burned in *Le Retour de Martin Guerre*, has his stomach blown away in *Fort Saganne*, plays a hunchback in *Jean de Florette* and has a nose that takes three hours daily to put on in *Cyrano de Bergerac*. It is to be hoped that he doesn't decide to delete these roles from his repertoire, as there are virtually no other leading men prepared to risk their popular image for a physically imperfect (i.e. undesirable) one. John Hurt did it in *The Elephant Man* but didn't hang around to do another half-dozen deformed roles after it. It is, generally speaking, dangerous screen territory. Perhaps Depardieu will tempt fate by doing a remake of his all-time hero Charles Laughton's 1939 classic *The Hunchback of Nôtre-Dame*.

As they completed filming La *Femme d'à Côté* in May 1981, François Mitterrand defeated Valéry Giscard d'Estaing and was elected President of France. Socialists wept for joy in the streets of Paris that night. Civil servants shredded documents. Old Gaullists sent back their Légion d'Honneur ribbons. The left might have been in decline in most other Western countries, but it was rising in France. For Depardieu, who had always despised politics and had never voted in a French election, it awakened a latent political consciousness he didn't know he possessed.

'I get the feeling,' he told *Newsweek* in 1987, 'that Mitterrand really cares about people. None of the other politicos gives a damn.'

In *Lettres Volées* he writes a letter to *Monsieur le Président* which starts charmingly, recounting how at a political evening organised by the (now) Minister of Culture Jack Lang, the lift had stuck and how he, Depardieu, had managed, with the help of a ladder, to release it. When the doors opened, inside were François and Danielle Mitterrand.

Depardieu's first impressions are of an extremely human man and he writes how impressed he felt. The letter continues in a schmaltzy tone to say how both men later told each other how much they admired one another and ends with Depardieu saying emotionally how Mitterrand, for whom he voted, was the sort of person one would like to have as a father or as a grandfather – or, indeed, as a president. He adds that anybody reading the letter would think he was the director of the Socialist Party campaign but, in fact, he says he doesn't understand politics at all and is not involved in them. Involved or not, however, one irreverent remark

Martin Guerre: strapping up to be hanged

Danton: head almost in basket

about his political idol and, in an instant, his face clouds with anger and confusion.

He seldom appears in political films. All his films have some sort of strong social comment, be it historical, like *Martin Guerre* and *Danton*, or society-based, like all the Blier and Pialat films, but few are directly political. In *Le Grand Frère* (*The Big Brother*) he sticks his neck out a little on the question of the French government's Arab policy, in *Fort Saganne* on the colonial question, and in *Uranos* the wartime Vichy government. But a political film rarely becomes popular with audiences unless it has somebody like Robert Redford in it (as in *All The President's Men, the* film about Watergate) or the whiff of sex and glamorous corruption, as in *Scandal*, about the Profumo affair. The mass audience in France tends to prefer thrills and laughs to realism, as the French box-office figures for 1991 show. Depardieu's most popular film is *La Chèvre* (*The Goat*), a breathtakingly fast comedy set in Mexico.

Depardieu was holidaying on Ile de Ré, off La Rochelle, when he received the script. He returned immediately to Paris to discuss it with Livi and happened to bump into actor Pierre Richard in the corridor at Artmedia. They chatted briefly and a few days later were sitting round a table with director Francis Veber discussing the project. Veber and Richard were old friends. Veber, whose screenwriting credits include *La Cage Aux Folles*, had written a film for him in 1972 called *Le Grand Blond avec une Chaussure Noire* (*The Tall Blond Man with One Black Shoe*). Richard had also starred in Veber's first directed film *Le Jouet* (*The Toy*) in 1976 which was turned into an American film starring Richard Pryor.

Depardieu joined the team later and instantly felt part of the family. In Mexico he and Richard shared an apartment, both having a horror of sleeping alone in strange hotel rooms. He told *Première* magazine's Marc Esposito, the journalist who has documented Depardieu's career from the start, that they knew everything there was to know about each other. With Veber, a man Depardieu sees as having a lost air about him, he developed an almost maternal sense of protection. At the end of shooting *La Chèvre* he sat back in total contentment and reckoned that he had at last found a *real* film family.

La Chèvre was the first of three hugely successful films – the other two being *Les Compères* (1983) and *Les Fugitifs* (1986) – Veber made in collaboration with Depardieu and Richard. *Les Compères* and *Les Fugitifs* currently rank fifth and sixth respectively on the Depardieu bestseller list. To describe them in a nutshell, it could be said that they are Keaton and Chaplin revisited with modern sophistication and Gallic charm. All three are based on the same formula: two men in search of a third, younger person.

In *La Chèvre*, the two men are searching for a teenage runaway (Corynne Charbit), a girl who has always attracted disaster and who finds herself, on arriving in Mexico, in the hands of criminals. Her agitated father (Michel Robin), an important Parisian businessman, immediately hires a detective called Campana (Depardieu) to find her. He fails spectacularly. On the advice of a psychic, her father also hires Perrin, an amiable bumbler (Richard, for whom physical comedy is something of a speciality), who is as maladroit as the girl. With hardly time to breathe, the two men 'take' Mexico by storm.

'By choosing a man as unlucky as the girl you hope he will step on the same banana peel as she did,' explains Veber, one of the few French directors to cross the Atlantic with professional success. 'To balance the clumsy you have to have the solid, the abstract and the mechanical, two actors with very different styles, like Depardieu and Richard.'

Veber has been frequently compared to Hollywood's Frank Capra, a man who shot the world through rose-coloured spectacles. Capra believed, rightly, that thousands of people all over the world wanted to look at it the same way, but with Veber there's also a hint of sadism. At the time he said that for a director to find a couple of actors like Richard and Depardieu was a real gift, more than reciprocated by the actors. The buddy-buddy screen duo they created is probably the best remembered in the history of French cinema. Their secret, says Depardieu, is that the comedy is never treated superficially. They play it with absolute seriousness.

'Comedy is the hardest thing because it is an exercise in humility.'

12

One-Man Film Industry at Home: Bougival

In 1982, Depardieu films accounted for nearly ten per cent of total French film revenue. That means that 1981 was the first of the truly great Depardieu years. By 1983 the good news had filtered through, as the Association des Cadres de l'Industrie Cinématographique, the French cinema managers' group, gave him their Prix ACIC for his body of work. He'd made a handful of solid, popular and some artistic hits, and the cameras were just about to roll on his most striking film to date, *Le Retour de Martin Guerre* (*The Return of Martin Guerre*).

Although Depardieu refuses to tag any film as representing the 'true Depardieu', twice in the 80s I heard him choose *Martin Guerre* as the film he relates to most, because of the character's ambiguity. Like Guerre on screen, off screen Depardieu can fall prey to the turbulent contradictions that he often displays so convincingly in his films. Indeed it was his powerful, peasant-like presence that the film focussed on.

The story of Martin Guerre, a sixteenth-century soldier and adventurer, is a romantic mystery that has fascinated people for four centuries. Its fascination stretches even across the Atlantic. Depardieu, with a naughty grin, tells of how Robert De Niro allegedly wanted to make the story into a film with himself as Guerre, Martin Scorsese directing and Meryl Streep in the role of Guerre's wife. According to his source, an American producer he met over a drink at a film festival, the De Niro team was actually in France scouting for locations when they learned about the Depardieu project.

The Martin Guerre story was first recorded by a Toulouse magistrate in the reign of François I, and was later the subject of novels, an operetta and an essay by Montaigne. It is the tale of a hefty country youth, who leaves his village, the hamlet of Artigat, and his child-bride of twelve, Bertrande, as a soldier and returns nine years later to a hero's welcome. Guerre resumes married life with the delighted Bertrande (Depardieu's long-standing screen partner, Nathalie Baye). Friends and family fall on him. The village is overjoyed to have him back. After his wartime experiences he is much maturer and able to be a good farmer, husband and father. He takes his role in the village structure, and he and Bertrande settle happily into a life with their children.

For Martin the years pass peacefully until a group of ex-soldiers pass through the village and hail him as their former comrade, Pansette. Told that he is Martin Guerre, they protest that they knew Martin, that he had fought with them and lost a leg in battle. The family shrug it off, but the village cobbler later finds Martin's foot is smaller than it used to be. Tongues begin to wag. When Martin and his uncle fall out over the profits of the family farm (Bertrande's dowry), the older man accuses him of being an imposter and raises a faction of supporters in the village before denouncing Martin to the provincial authorities. Witnesses are found who will identify him as Pansette, and he is arrested and taken to Toulouse; there he is put on trial for his life. And then a new witness arrives – the man with only one leg.

'The subject of *Martin Guerre* is: what harm is there in making happy a woman whose husband has abandoned her?' comments Depardieu. 'These days people are more tied up with divorce proceedings than making their marriage succeed.'

It is an extraordinary costume drama which chronicles village life and the mood of the times, and has a sense of period that you can almost smell. Filled with twists and suspense, the final courtroom scene ranks as one of the cinema's great cliffhangers, with Depardieu, sporting a Joan of Arc haircut and beard, giving a beautifully executed performance of controlled power and ennobling tragedy. Director Daniel Vigne recounts how Depardieu, being *un terrien* (an earthlover), immediately felt at ease with the subject and slid into the role as if he were born into it.

Nathalie Baye described her co-star as being utterly fascinated by Guerre's intelligence, fieriness and madness. Baye, as Bertrande, with her hair pushed under a scarf, clad in beige and brown, could have been one of those young women working the field in the paintings of Le Nain or Breughel. Like

Defending his life in Martin Guerre, *1982*

Depardieu, she had worked with the best contemporary directors of France – Pialat, Blier and Truffaut – and made her mark on French audiences. With *Martin Guerre* she was about to become a name abroad.

'It was such a strong story,' she says. 'Two people living such intense love which, between them, was total. It is very rare to find something like that. For us it was one of those films that was sheer magic to make. Magnificent scenery, a wonderful village, beautiful costumes and a harmony on set. We were all *très en forme*! We felt so relaxed making the film that when we took off our costumes in the evenings and changed into jeans and jumpers we felt like we were getting *into* costume.'

The film became an art-house blockbuster in Britain and in America, where it was nominated for an Oscar. But it didn't do much in France, wasn't selected for Cannes and never got a mention at the Césars. It was a snub that marked the start of quite a long period when the French critics went off Depardieu. Perhaps he had become such a fixture on the French scene that he was taken for granted at home. Long before America 'discovered' him in 1990 with *Cyrano, Green Card* and the rape scandal, he said stoically, 'the French critics hardly even mention me any more'. He was reacting to a considerable backlash to his success and charges of over-exposure. People said he was over-used: writing a guest column in *Le Nouvel Observateur*, renowned Paris civil rights lawyer Denis Laglois compared Depardieu to Bogart; 'Bogart bothers me because his presence erases the hero he is playing. I have the same problem with Depardieu, whom I've recently seen everywhere. I can't stand any more of him.' At one point the criticism became so bad that the actor took a long sabbatical and disappeared with Elisabeth to South America.

Rejection and jealousy often happen when people peak in showbusiness. The same happened to John Travolta in the early 80s after the fabulous success of *Saturday Night Fever* and *Grease*. That is not, for sure, the reason why Travolta and Depardieu became such close friends, although both were worked over by the press, particularly *Time* magazine – Depardieu for the rape scandal, Travolta for his commitment to Scientology – but it must have added some weight to their friendship. They also have distinct personal similarities. Each gives the appearance of being in a state of suspended adolescence and both still affect the air of naughty boys observing the world. Each has been described as 'a young Marlon Brando'. Both fell for older women – Travolta's big love was the late actress Diana Hyland, thirteen years his senior – and both easily balloon into fat.

While in London promoting Brian da Palma's thriller *Blow Out*, Travolta mentioned to me that he'd just returned from Paris where he'd been visiting the Depardieus. He'd flown himself over in his twin-engine, six-seater Cessna Citation with only a co-pilot. It had taken just eleven hours from California, where he has an estate above Santa Barbara, to the French capital. He was as chuffed about it all as a kid with a pocketful of sweets.

'I first saw Gérard act in *Going Places* [*Les Valseuses*] about six years ago and became a fan,' he said. 'Then, years later, when I was free, I heard he was shooting a film on the outskirts of Paris. I flew in and went up to him and said: "I wanted to meet you, I'm such a fan of yours." He was quite overwhelmed by this. My French is as bad as his English but we managed.' (Depardieu has been quoted as saying that they overcome the language barrier by 'communicating through the soul'.) 'Anyway, we became friends. I think we have a similar appeal and a world of things could happen for us. We are talking of doing a comedy together, in French, with Catherine Deneuve!'

The Depardieus later visited Travolta's ranch to swim, ride, watch old movies and eat meals prepared by Depardieu (a passionate cook who specialises in country dishes like *bœuf en daube*, *pâté de foie gras* and *coq au vin*). Each time Depardieu goes to America he heads for Santa Barbara. So far, their comedy in French hasn't appeared; the press has, however, linked Travolta romantically with Deneuve, and his friendship with Elisabeth and Gérard Depardieu has grown. One of the guest rooms in the Bougival home is, say the Depardieus, for their visiting 'brother', Travolta. Depardieu's English has improved considerably with the making of *Green Card* and Travolta's French is now quite passable.

One anecdote told by publicist Pamela Godfrey involving them both, however, reveals the dangers of being too casual with fame. During Travolta's promotional trip to Europe with *Blow Out* in 1982, he spent a free day at home with Elisabeth and Gérard. It was his twenty-seventh birthday. The Depardieus had baked a cake. John and Gérard spent the day working out together in the gym, playing football on the lawn, singing round the piano and generally having a good time *en famille*. With them was a friend, a well-known French photographer, who snapped it all 'for the album'. He also sold the pictures to *Paris-Match*, and soon Depardieu and Travolta, dressed in Depardieu's oldest work-out gear – grey for John, purple for Gérard – were laid out liberally across several double-page spreads.

Photographs of the two stars gambolling in unbelievably tatty tracksuits full of holes would, under normal circumstances, be perfectly acceptable; but Filmways, the distributor of *Blow Out*, had put together a multi-million publicity campaign for Travolta. On the insistence of his (then) personal manager Bob LeMond, Travolta always had to look 'a star' and wear expensive designer clothes in public. Both parties, understandably, were shattered at the sheer immaturity of their star – and at his friend, who should have known better.

However, in France the public are less star-struck than in Britain and North America. Depardieu *can* still walk down a street without being mobbed by fans or eat out at a restaurant in peace. He is still comparatively free of the invisible barriers that fame throws up between actor and public. Yet for somebody who claims to want to keep his private life private, Depardieu hasn't even begun to practise what he preaches.

The Depardieu home in Bougival has been featured in house-and-garden magazines, interviews are carried out there, as are family photo sessions. At his château in Anjou on the edge of the Loire Valley, television camera crews have waded their way around making documentaries and glossy magazines feature glowing accounts of his life as a *vigneron* (winemaker). Even their sanctuary, a villa in Trouville is well known.

The Bougival home is made up of three houses, the original, bought in 1977, plus two neighbouring ones acquired later. For the first few years the family camped in a couple of rooms in the original house, Elisabeth dealing with the builders while Gérard was away making movies. Gradually the place expanded into a sprawling home built on three levels. The houses cluster together in a lavish, curved garden full of climbing wisteria and fruit trees, lawns and roses. Gérard says he'd like to be buried there under the wisteria.

Inside, the house is old, low-beamed and comfortably rambling, filled with plants, bric-à-brac and souvenirs from various roles. Abandoned clothes dot the chairs like wrecked cushions. Elegant antiques mix with old country furniture they've picked up on trips away from Paris scouring village shops for bargains. Elisabeth loves things from the end of the nineteenth century; he prefers a more rural touch. The walls are covered with unusual oils and engravings, and in their bedroom there's a Corot.

The style of the Depardieu home is largely due to Elisabeth, who adores renovating and restoring fabrics and furnishings and, over the years as wife and mother, has made a place which fits the idea of a family home. They have a music room where she and Guillaume, now a music-college student, practise. Gérard has a study, complete with a new set of freshly bound encyclopaedias. Julie has her own quarters. The relationship between parents and offspring reflects a harmonious family. Guillaume, blond and tall with his mother's generous mouth and a modified version of his father's nose, is co-starring with Gérard in a film, the son playing the father as a young man. Julie is training to be a designer and looks like a younger version of her mother, has inherited from her father a love of tattoos and plans to design a book with him.

Like a lot of successful, preoccupied men, Depardieu appears to have been an affectionate and indulgent father, but often a very distant one. 'I think I was too young to have children back in my twenties,' he sighs. 'They are lucky in their mother but a father like me is a total handicap. Guillaume is very mature for his age, very discreet and he doesn't like publicity. Celebrity is really not his trip. Julie is very beautiful because she loves life and is so strong, so assured.

'As a parent I am worried because the world is worse than it used to be. Before, it was alcohol, now it's drugs. I never took LSD in the 60s because I am, above all, a traveller and I don't need artificial stimulants to help me on my way. I don't know if Guillaume has tried them – perhaps he has – but I have warned him: "You can try everything, but then there will be nothing left to do." '

He has always said that he doesn't want his children ever to experience the isolating childhood emotions he had and seems, so far, to have succeeded. When filming near home he has been known to take time off to attend parent-teacher meetings at the schools of his children. (Frequently the other parents stared at him with hostility due to the controversial nature of some of his films.) But most films are shot on location. Short of bundling up the family and taking them with him, as he did when they were young, there is no way round the fact that his work means a family split.

Family life at home centres on the kitchen, which is enormous. There Gérard cooks vast meals for family and friends – 'I'm a homeboy not a playboy' – anything from Chinese to Berrichois, and loads of puddings, as in *le pudding*. The image of him in *Green Card* as the cholesterol-high, food-mad Frenchman who crushes a bulb of garlic with his bare hands is not so far from the real McCoy. A fanatical *gourmet*, it is said that when he's filming he cultivates the location chef like other actors cultivate the director, and takes his own recipes on set with him. On bad days he can usually be found in the on-set kitchen wagon, nibbling away at the pot. He has even been known to follow a savoury smell, track it down to the kitchen of some modest home in an unknown village, knock on the door and ask to have a taste.

And then, of course, there's the wine cellar, one of the best-stocked private cellars in the land. He became interested in fine wines and wine-making about ten years ago, and has since made up for lost time, collecting and storing in his cellar thousands of bottles of the world's greatest vintages.

Then there's also the daily, the gardener and the man who drives Depardieu to appointments when he's not going by motorbike. (When his boss lost his driving licence for six months in 1990 he drove him in Depardieu's 1977 Mercedes Benz. Depardieu was reportedly fined £1,000 on a drunk-driving charge which he said happened while he was fiddling with the car radio on a country road near Vichy.) Across the road from *chez* Depardieu, his sister Hélène lives with her husband, production director Patrick Bordier, and works for her brother as his secretary. D.D. Productions, his film company, is based in the house at Bougival.

It appears to be very cordial down at Bougival-sur-Seine, Paris's equivalent of Kingston-on-Thames. Since the children have grown up Elisabeth has managed to forge a new career for herself as a *chanteuse*. With her partner François Bernheim, she has put on shows in Paris and has, since

Driving

the early 80s, also run a small theatre troupe in Bougival. Her acting classes are very *de rigueur* in this two-café, one-restaurant village. Clearly a feisty, tolerant but firm woman, she seems to have survived admirably, living in the shadow of her husband, with his complex mix of talent and restlessness. She has never let herself be belittled as an individual. She might be *petite*, pretty and perfectly Parisian, but she is no porcelain doll. There is a spine of steel and a sense that this woman is mistress of her own life. Characterising the two of them in musical terms, she calls Gérard 'a rock opera, a mixture of tragic violence and a most refined sense of expression', and herself as a 'ballad'.

When they invited *Time* magazine home (in 1984, well before the rape scandal) to snap them at ease for a cover story, she played along in a charming way, posing as the retiring wife pouring him coffee but couldn't resist teasing, in a confident jest: 'This is what you'd really like, isn't it? A dutiful wife fixing your morning coffee!'

At the time, there was gossip in Paris that the couple might have been thrashing out the inevitable stresses of fame and life in public. In 1991, to counter rumours that they had split up, they posed at their Trouville home for a romantic colour spread which appeared in magazines worldwide.

'I found him. He's mine and I'm keeping him,' Elizabeth is quoted as saying.

'We might have our own *fracas*,' he says, 'but it's like anybody else and we only have them at home. We have an intelligent rapport. Of course we have our highs and lows, but Elisabeth is the woman of my life.'

He is game for a little seductive teasing but he says he values fidelity over flirtation. 'Conquest is not heroic,' he says. 'What's heroic is making love last.' They have an intangibly picaresque panache about them as a couple, even though one knows that with actors nothing is what it may seem.

13

Hanging in the Balance

One of the most disquieting trends in France in the 1980s was the blatant increase in racism, directed mainly at the nation's two million-plus immigrants, mostly Arabs from former North African colonies. When Depardieu, the public's hero, chose to make *Le Grand Frère*, a controversial and violent family drama about the victimisation of immigrant Arabs, co-starring with a largely Arab cast, he was going against the grain. Peasants and gangsters, yes; Arabs, no.

When it came out, the film, made with an appropriately dry realism treating an explosive contemporary political theme, was coolly received, possibly because it came out in summer, when half of France is away on holiday and virtually all of Paris has moved to the country. Filmed in free time between *Martin Guerre* and *Danton*, it was shot largely in Marseilles and Africa, and is based on American writer Sam Ross's novel, *Ready for the Tiger*. Francis Girod again directed Depardieu in what film buffs described as a sort of Jean Gabin role. (This Gabin/Depardieu comparison has irritated Depardieu; once at a press conference, when asked what he felt about always being compared with Jean Gabin, he snapped back that Gabin had never played Duras!) Alain Delon was going to play the 'big brother', but both the politics and the fact that there was violence against children in it made him withdraw. Depardieu said the story made him think of *Night of the Hunter*, a curious film made in 1955 with Laughton and Robert Mitchum (another of Depardieu's favourite actors) about a fanatical preacher pitted against the forces of innocent children.

110

The big brother with immigrant 'sister' Souad Amidou, 1982

Le Grand Frère starts with Depardieu (acting a character once again named Gérard) and a fellow pilot (Jean Rochefort) crashing in Sierra Leone. Betrayed by the pilot and left for dead, Gérard revives and returns to France as Bernard, a man with a score to settle but who becomes involved in something alien to him, the Arab sub-culture which lives and dies behind half-closed doors throughout France. He moves in with Ali (Hakim Ghanem), a boy of thirteen, and his older sister Zina (Souad Amidou) in their dry, dusty shack on the coast near Marseilles, near their awkward 'uncle', who's not as kindly as he at first appears.

'What seduced me into making this film,' said Depardieu, 'was the possibility of showing on screen the milieu of the immigrant, the people who live *au bout du port* [at the bottom of society's pile], what it's like for them.' Deep down, he must have felt that it had been like that for his rural parents 'immigrating' to the suburbs of Châteauroux. It was what he had left behind, the corpse over which he had pulled a sheet. Always on the side of the minority, the outcasts, the dispossessed, Depardieu, the eternal immigrant, an immigrant from the interior, fighting on the screen rather than on the streets, expressed this message. Now, as a star, somebody who employs a driver to take him home when he's too exhausted to make it alone, he does it without losing face.

As 1983 dawned, Depardieu's second costume drama, *Danton*, opened in Paris with him playing an effete Georges Danton, the pleasure-loving lawyer who becomes a leader of the French Revolution.

'I'd like to do more historical films,' he said. 'They illuminate the present. But sadly the French cinema doesn't have the money to produce spectacular epic movies.' (Ironically *Martin Guerre* and *Danton* together won him the Best Actor of the Year award from the Association of American Critics.) *Danton* was a Polish–French co-production. A brilliant, brooding film by Polish director (now a Senator in the Polish government) Andrzej Wajda, it was made in Paris (Wajda had wanted to make it in Poland but political upheavals prevented it) with a Franco–Polish cast and crew. Instructions to crew and actors had to be repeated in Polish, French, German and Italian, as no two languages sufficed to communicate the director's wishes and the entire production became an epic in its own right.

Based on a 1930s Polish play, the film covers the months between the summer of 1793 and April 1794, when the Revolution was divided by internal and foreign influences. It was a time when duelling revolutionaries, Danton and Robespierre, were at each other's throats in the cut and thrust of the new Republic. The title role for Depardieu was generally considered to be so far beyond his range that word got out that he had finally cracked. However, people tend to underestimate him. Along with Jean de Florette and Martin Guerre, it is his most powerful role to date. The film was met, however, by a cool-to-hostile reception from both officialdom and the press in his home country. It was nominated in the 1983 Césars for Best Film and Best Actor but won neither. (Best Actor went to Philippe Léotard for *La Balance*.)

Talking about the role he told Martyn Auty of *Time Out*: 'You could say there are two aspects to my character that I'm still struggling to contain: the animal and the infantile. Danton had these qualities too, so I guess I'm working them out through my performances. He had a streak of childishness; like me, he was committed to the pursuit of pleasure and he was a great performer too – an orator of considerable stature with a voice to match. I like to think he had my mischievous sense of humour too.'

Depardieu read half a dozen books on Danton before starting on the film, but also attributes his inspiration for the character as coming from his visits to Poland to see director Andrzej Wajda. Wajda had conceived the idea of a film on Danton long before Solidarity and long before martial law, and Depardieu had visited him there in those early days.

'What struck me most was the atmosphere of exhaustion and euphoria

Danton: *before the guillotine*

among the Polish people. When you're excessively tired you become very clear-sighted. It was this quality I wanted to bring out in Danton.'

His Danton is popular, earthy, sybaritic and belching, swaggeringly over-confident and fuelled with animal cunning. His struggle for mastery is with the authoritarian Maximilien de Robespierre, supervisor of the machinery of terror run by the zealous Committee for Public Safety. Played by Polish actor Wojciech Pszoniak (dubbed from Polish into French), Robespierre is a cold, sickly man with a face like a hatchet and a conscience so authoritarian that he is driven to strike by principle. Parallels between Lech Walesa and General Jaruzelski were there for the taking.

'Danton believes that the fruits of victory had to be enjoyed, whereas Robespierre opted for perpetual revolution, in the Trotskyite fashion,' comments Depardieu. 'Danton obviously has blood on his hands; he's sent a lot of people to the guillotine, but he believes in *life.*'

In the film we see him relishing just that, mixing with prostitutes, guzzling at banquets and quaffing liberally – until he, like so many others facing their inevitable destiny, is sent to the guillotine by Robespierre.

'To play the role of Danton, the heart and the spirit of the French Revolution, I thought of Muhammad Ali. I know him and I've been around him. One day I saw him go to sleep at the dinner table. He just sat there and – *hup* – suddenly he's off. And I thought, "That's good for Danton." I watched the way Ali walks around, whistles, the way he's there, a presence, but he's not really there: the way he's in control, but not really in control. And I thought, "This is all good for Danton: these images are very important. The power and the strength." They both [Danton and Ali] had these things but *still* got KO'd.' At the time of shooting Depardieu apparently was suffering from extreme fatigue – and the effects of a binge. 'I was dead-drunk for weeks,' he says. 'I didn't sleep, I wanted to experience a sense of fatigue in my movements and speech, as Danton would have felt in 1793. It amused me to do it, it was interesting to discover one's limits. Writers like Rimbaud and Baudelaire did the same sort of thing.

'To play the part of Danton I kept on getting completely drunk and overate for six weeks, and couldn't stop being drunk until it was all over. At one point it has to stop, but you have to get on with it and that's tough. Maybe I'm overdoing it, but it is in fact professional behaviour. It's really quite normal. I'm often accused of overdoing it, but people don't see the difference between "overdone" and "abundant". When one is overdoing it, it is distracting. But with abundance, it's not.'

In the run-up to his climactic, final confrontation, when Danton delivers a long, impassioned speech, Depardieu was so tired he was close to collapse. The crew and 600 extras were visibly uneasy as Wajda attempted to persuade his star to rest before filming.

'I know what I'm doing!' screamed Depardieu. 'I know what I'm capable of!' He hit his mark, started the speech, the cameras rolled and only one take was needed. Everybody breathed silent sighs of relief. He had the power and the strength, but felt quite knocked out at the end of it.

'I like working with Depardieu,' said Wadja. 'He is a great actor who has the ability to create violence from within. He can make something extraordinary.'

This sense of violence is something that has been one of the great Depardieu enigmas. It is one of his favourite interview topics. He says he doesn't need power but does need violence.

'Violence can be a positive way of communication, power only crushes.' He uses what he calls the 'pun' of the word *violer*, which means 'to rape' or 'violate' in the sense of a bad director 'raping' a film; in early days, he allowed screeds of his half-digested (or mistranslated) philosophy about violence to be printed in the production notes of some of his films or in the profiles released by Unifrance, France's government-backed organisation to promote French films abroad.

Much of it is in philosophical *non sequiturs* but clearly there is a deep-seated frustration and struggle to tame his basic instinctive violence. It is rather like Lenny, the gentle giant in *Of Mice and Men*, who keeps rabbits and breaks women's necks when he tries to stroke their hair because he is unable to contain or communicate his emotion. Depardieu can bellow like a bull and charge around the room far more easily than sitting down and talking about it. He doesn't believe in machismo and emanates a strange, childish sweetness from his invisible world. Yet with an almost imperceptible twitch of a facial muscle he can switch from an irresistible, vulnerable innocent to an aggressive, obsessive, unpredictable thug. The grey eyes can blacken so dangerously that one glances round for a place to hide.

I noticed this the first time I saw Depardieu in the flesh at the Cannes film festival in 1983. He wasn't, as everybody else said, 6' 2"; more like 5' 11" and growing – outwards. *Danton* hadn't yet opened in Britain and *La Lune Dans le Caniveau* (*The Moon in the Gutter*) was being shown at the festival. The first film made by Jean-Jacques Beineix since his celebrated *Diva*, and starring Nastassja Kinski and Depardieu, it had been booed and whistled off the screen. At a small press conference afterwards a young woman reporter who had obviously seen neither *Martin Guerre* nor *Le Dernier Métro*, nor read the press release on the film, asked Depardieu what other films he'd made. This most undignified of questions justifiably infuriated him – with forty-eight behind him then there was no easy answer. Depardieu does not suffer fools gladly and he blasted her almost out of the room. His eyes were dark, and his whole body flared in rage like a toad does when frightened. A few seconds later he was the smiling blond with the shaggily cut hair, black *blouson* and good-natured giggle again. It was exactly this ability to change in a split second that made Beineix choose Depardieu for his film.

'I was interested in doing something that I could only do with someone who had a certain image and would agree to question it. Depardieu was obviously the only one amongst all the stars I knew of. He has always done violence to his image. He had the ideal personality for the role: a mixture of enormous power and immense frailty.'

During that Cannes festival, Depardieu, who hated the film, told one interviewer with characteristic bluntness that *The Moon* was 'a police movie preoccupied with its navel' and he was 'an actor in an idiot of a movie'. He added, with his well-known slight sniff, head turned back and hair floating, 'The moon might be in the gutter but the movie is in the sewer'.

The film, based on a novel by David Goodis, features Depardieu as a hulking, deranged and haunted stevedore (again called Gérard), the brother of a young woman who has cut her throat after being raped in a dead-end alley in the docks. At the time of her tragedy, he is lying in a hospital bed in a narcotic fog. Once his head has cleared he goes out endlessly seeking his sister's rapist. One night he meets wealthy beauty Loretta (Kinski) who promises to take him away from the gutter and find a solution to his quest. Kinski called him her 'strongest [screen] partner'. He didn't call her anything.

'Go, go, go!' Beineix would shout, and Depardieu went on to describe how hard the director had driven the cast, stars and extras alike. 'He made *The Moon* only to please himself. I don't make movies that way. I don't work to please only one person, even if it is the director.'

Depardieu apparently felt that things were not always under control. 'The bullets were always coming at you and you had to dodge all the time. Well, you didn't *have* to dodge – but I prefer to live.' He also said how much he liked the books of David Goodis, but not the treatment this one received.

Would he work with Beineix again? 'It depends. One experience doesn't make a life. I don't hold grudges,' he replies.

But Depardieu, at that time, didn't really care. He was about to join up with his buddies Francis Veber and Pierre Richard for situation comedy *Les Compères* (*Father's Day*), their second screen outing together. D.D. Productions, along with Pierre Richard's company Fideline Films, were co-producing along with Veber's Efvé Films, and apart from having some fun together, they were intent on making something for their most devoted audience – the French public who loved comedy that redefined adolescence.

Again the three of them lived in the same house during the shooting of the film, sat reading their scenarios together, ate, drank and had silly photos taken of them doing silly things together. Depardieu did the cooking as

Les Compères, *1983, with 'class mate' Pierre Richard*

Veber, known for his lack of domesticity, 'nearly blew up the kitchen'. They were, as the crinkly haired Richard said, a trio without clashes, without egos. Together, Veber remarked, Richard and Depardieu had the effect 'of water on freeze-dried coffee', with the powder the script whooshing into flavoursome coffee when the water was added.

'With Pierrot and Francis it was like being three boys at a private school doing a project together,' says Depardieu. 'Francis was the one who was third or fourth in class and passed you slips of paper to help you during the test, and you helped him outside in the playground. Pierrot was the dunce, and I was the bad smell, the one who had to fart to be noticed at all.'

Eight years after it was released, *Les Compères* still stood fifth on the list of Depardieu's most popular films. (He flew from a location in Mauretania where he was shooting *Fort Saganne* for the film's opening in Paris and was reported saying jubilantly: 'We clicked 35,000 tickets the first day. It's sublime!')

In *Les Compères* Richard and Depardieu play two men who are both told separately by the same woman (who is lying) that they have fathered her teenage son, Tristan (Stéphane Bierry). The boy has run away to join a gang of *voyous* and the girl he loves, and, as the lover's conventional husband makes little effort to find him, she hopes to con both men into doing so. But along the way, both would-be fathers find themselves warming to the idea of paternity as they step deeper and deeper into an improbable stew. What would have been a tragedy for French society – the broken family – twenty-five years earlier was now being shown as farce.

Depardieu plays Jean Lucas, a high-powered newspaper reporter-cum-soft-guy (the straight man again), and Richard, with his high-browed clown's face, plays a manic depressive, François Pignon. As in *La Chèvre* they are a modern, French Laurel and Hardy, a grotesque comedy version of Danton and Robespierre.

'It is easy to be dramatic and violent on screen,' said Depardieu of Lucas, 'but it is much harder to be a prototype like Lucas, who is tender and caring. You need to find humility and passion in yourself. What I loved about him was the goodwill he put into his machismo. He almost gives it an allegorical vision.'

Although situation, script and slapstick made this both a hilariously funny and reassuring film, there was, of course, a hidden moral about finding out about your child and about yourself. Depardieu apparently found himself pondering a more balanced view of paternity and of the needs of children.

'My children,' he reflects, 'sometimes look at me like I'm a crazy man.'

14

Camels and Cops

Depardieu is rarely cast opposite a typical *fille fatale*, pouting lips, smoking eyes, undone blouses and all. Being so *fatal* himself, he is no doubt the sex symbol of his life; also, possibly because a young slip of a size-eight girl, all legs, quivering lips and cheekbones, would look dangerously vulnerable next to his pillar of flesh, with his rough gait and rougher hands. He tends to spark better on screen with the more innocent peasant looks of, for example, Nathalie Baye in *Martin Guerre*, or the sophistication of Deneuve or Ardant – or perhaps somebody with a mouth that looks as though it can do a great blow job.

In *Fort Saganne* (1984) they tried to see if he could work with *une fille fatale*. Depardieu was Charles Saganne, a French Foreign Legionnaire who helped bring the Sahara under French rule in the early 1900s. Looking succulently debonair in a Beau Geste *casquette* and flowing white desert robes, he plays one of his more starry roles. Galumphing around in the cruel sun on camels in vast desert sweeps and shimmering oases definitely suits him. Although the lovely Deneuve was also there in the torrid heat as a chic, cool, feminist journalist who turns nurse (in full make-up and hairdo straight from Paris), it is the poutingly pubescent Sophie Marceau, then sixteen (who had risen to fame aged thirteen in *La Boum*, France's first and only brat-pack movie), whom Depardieu is passionately pitted against. Marceau plays Madeleine de Sainte-Ilette, the elegant and educated daughter of the director of a large Franco-Algerian company, who, despite the constant chaperonage of her mother, falls madly in love with Saganne.

Fort Saganne: *screen love, Sophie Marceau*

Perhaps because of their lack of screen chemistry, Marceau and Depardieu's wooing didn't work at all; or because, as Marceau says, he was 'so protective, like a big brother', that the male/female thing between them was so flat on celluloid. The film, however, remains a high-budget spectacular epic to watch, sumptuously photographed by Bruno Nuytten.

Saganne is an officer facing the consequences of a military cock-up. He's typically individualistic, an old-fashioned hero who becomes aware of the limitations of military values in the colonial wars. Killed in the trenches in the First World War, he had a Foreign Legion outpost named after him. Philippe Noiret plays the colonel who orders him south, and sets up the ridiculous game of discipline and rule. The film was shot in a Mauretanian village called Chinguetti, 'the seventh holy city of Islam', under the direction of Alain Corneau of *Choix des Armes*. Depardieu's early mentor Jean-Laurent Cochet played a politician and 90s matinée idol Hippolyte Giradot had the part of a cello-playing desert doctor.

Journalist William Blaylock, who travelled there with them, describes

Depardieu arriving at Dakar airport when the actor's mood shifted from 'playful to crass with the speed of a sandstorm'.

'I hate barriers, I hate laws,' declared Depardieu, to the surprised Senegalese border policeman which resulted in the actor's being put temporarily into custody. On his release, fifteen minutes later, he laughed. 'I didn't think he was going to get so mad.'

Later, during a stopover at Nouakchott, en route to Chinguetti, he blandly ignored passport control and sped off to a faded hotel to buy four cold beers which he downed noisily on the plane. Finally on set, in temperatures well over a hundred degrees under the arc lamps, he was, by all accounts, uncomplaining and professional. A crew member remarks: 'It's never dull with Depardieu because you never know what the bugger is going to do. It can be very upsetting working with him but he always know his lines and hits his mark when "action" is called. Then, when not on call, he goes off into the middle of the desert and gets blotto on a huge forty-eight-hour bender.'

The film is an anachronistic apology for France's imperial past, spiced with the romanticism of the old 30s French sagas. Writers on the history of French cinema continue to be surprised at the virtual absence of films about the colonial wars that divided the country and were directly responsible for the collapse of the Fourth Republic in 1958. There have been films about Foreign Legion activities but they are the traditional swashbuckling drama and desert-romance sort, blatantly imperialist in spirit. The French have still not been bold enough to confront topical colonial matters cinematically. Bertrand Tavernier's *Coup de Torchon* (*Clean Slate*), the story of a police chief in French West Africa during the 1930s, is perhaps the best-known French film to deal with colonialism.

Fort Saganne is an unsettled mix of moral tale and high-action exotica but then, as Francis Veber remarked, 'you can't make a left-wing colonial film'. Shooting it must have been sheer hell with the stifling heat and sand storms, the vast band of unskilled extras and the enormous distances involved in getting from one location to another. Depardieu, who finds the sun hard to bear, observed: 'In the Sahara you cannot move the way you do in the city. You have to yield, accept, or the sun will kill you. It changes you. You mustn't act or you would break up. You have to simply *be* the character.' In temperatures like those they were working in, he actually preferred the outside scenes to the stifling inside ones, and found the camels 'great company', an asset he attributes to their great stupidity, unlike horses which, by contrast, make him very nervous. Marguerite

Fort Saganne: *first love, the camels, 1984*

Duras, when asked what she thought of him in the film, replied: '*Fort Saganne*? He didn't do anything; he sat on a camel.' Depardieu, however, claims deeper motivation: 'I made *Fort Saganne* for a social reason. I try to go for the idea which will enable me to communicate the most and this one said something that I felt about the evil of colonialism.'

Hardly a month after completing *Fort Saganne*, Depardieu, with freckles and bleached blond hair, was back on stage, in Strasbourg, cranking theatrical machinery again in a preview run of Molière's satire on hypocrisy, *Le Tartuffe*. He had not been on the boards for six years, since Claude Régy's staging of Peter Handke's *Unreasonable People Are Dying Out.*

Some say Depardieu is difficult. Others say he's like a lamb. Crews and colleagues inevitably adore him, and co-stars laud his acting generosity. Naturally, as head of an interesting and successful film company that actors, directors and technicians would like to work for, French filmfolk are chary of commenting on his difficult – or unpredictable – side. When confronted in an interview by the statement, 'You have a reputation for being difficult', he has responded with sincere surprise. He doesn't think he's difficult, but admits that maybe sometimes he has been. He adds with his throaty laugh: 'There are always legends surrounding great actors, so perhaps I should take all this as a compliment if people say such things about me! . . . I like to drink, I like to play about. I like lots of stuff, but I'm not difficult. When we shoot, we shoot. I always work. When a movie is being shot, it becomes a battleground. That's just the way it is: shooting a film is war. But I find that from my position in the middle of the battleground it is very interesting. All directors are interesting, even the most stupid, the most idiotic. They all have their qualities and their defects. You accept those and work with them – just as they have to do with mine.

'They're always afraid, in a panic, always thinking you're leaving them. The relationship between an actor and a director is like a love story between a man and a woman. Sometimes I don't know who is the man and who is the woman. I'm sure sometimes I'm the woman. The director becomes more and more macho with the actors and I get like a woman, saying, "Oh, I don't understand. What is he trying to do to me?"'

'Making a movie I always learn something. I learn because I always have to fight. I am not a diplomat. It's the way people look at me that's difficult. If they want to give me a hard time, well . . . If they want to fight, I'll fight. I don't care.'

Depardieu had a chance to experience the problems of being a director first-hand when *Le Tartuffe* finished its run in Paris and he did an about-face to make a film version of the piece. Helming the production, with his wife as co-star and his money at stake, the project, which took three years to produce, provided the grounds to test how difficult he could be. The project, however, survived, was released and still crops up at film festivals where it is revered as a classy curiosity.

Depardieu decided to make the film himself as he didn't want the television cameras to come in and 'rape' the work. He'd actually wanted to make a film about actors, rehearsing, egos, acting and over-acting, but found he didn't have the time or patience for what he considered his 'very pretentious idea', and settled for a solidly faithful translation of director François Lassalle's production for the Théâtre National de Strasbourg, which transferred to Paris' Théâtre de la Ville in February 1984. In it Depardieu plays Tartuffe, Molière's hypocritical religious sensualist in a holier-than-thou guise, a handsome evil genius who worms his way into the bourgeois household of Orgon (François Périer) and almost succeeds in paupering its inhabitants.

Two weeks into rehearsal, when Isabelle Weingarten had to drop out because of ill-health, Elisabeth Depardieu took the role of Elmire, one of the targets of Tartuffe's desires. It marked the first time since 1971 that husband and wife had acted together. *Variety* described Depardieu as having 'uncommon acting ability... He stalks the premises like a warning phantom, a pale, gaunt figure cloaking his machinations with feigned piety. There is a smouldering intensity to his performance that holds the house.'

'I read the play just like any other script and found it very lively and quite cinematographic,' Depardieu says in the production notes of his film. 'I never studied *Tartuffe* at school, so my head wasn't stuffed with scholastic interpretations. I don't understand the footnotes you usually find in text-books or the questions and answers that are suggested. But I do understand the weight of words: what Tartuffe says, the way he digs himself into Orgon's house. 'I wanted to "save" a classical play so that people would remember it as a whole and avoid those awful "selected extracts" you see on TV. They remind one of a kind of Tussaud Museum.

'After two weeks of rehearsal Périer and I were a bit lost. We didn't *feel* the characters very well and we couldn't make our way through all the notes. We were sitting in a *brasserie* and had drunk a little when, all of a sudden, Périer started to tell me the story of Molière's problem with his wife and his lover.

'At one go, everything was clear and I said to myself: "That's just what we ought to shoot!" I remember that night well. We were in Strasbourg, near the cathedral and it was snowing. There wasn't even a cat running down the road. Périer kept on slipping, and I held his arm so he wouldn't fall down. I knew that this was what we had to express in the film. Express what is impossible to say with words. Pialat always tries to film such fugitive moments. As an actor, I try to do so myself.'

In a way, *Le Tartuffe* encompassed everything Depardieu had learned along the way from the TNP and his mentors through to the finer points of interpretation and the basics of film-making. Although it was the screen that brought him success and fame, his love of the stage and the classics had never cooled, just been put on hold. He revelled in being back on stage, performing nightly, and as soon as *Le Tartuffe* was in the can, he talked of doing the same with Molière's *Don Juan*.

His first screen character after *Le Tartuffe* was the suave solicitor in *Rive Droite Rive Gauche* (*Right Bank–Left Bank*), a romance set in '*bon chic-bon genre*' Paris. He and Nathalie Baye play yuppies who have had enough of striving in the '*BC–BG*' mire and decide to revolt. He is a Parisian

Depardieu as Tartuffe, 1984

With François Périer between rehearsals of Le Tartuffe, *1984*

lawyer, she a publicist who decides her business is as corrupt as his. He meets her, a thinking divorcee, at a gallery opening and falls for her, despite his supremely elegant bourgeoise wife Babée, played by Carole Bouquet. A little along the lines of Bertrand Blier's later Depardieu-starrer *Trop Belle Pour Toi* (*Too Beautiful For You*), where the elegant and bourgeoise wife Florence (also played by Bouquet) is forsaken for the plump and cosy Josianne Balasko, this version of gentrified French life was impeccably up to date. The notion of Depardieu – who for so long had worked on his image as a working-class rebel – as an upwardly mobile lawyer in Christian Dior suits is hard to swallow but, as the film progressed, it grows on one.

Director Philippe Labro, one-time novelist, journalist and TV anchorman, must have also had moments of unease about this unusual casting. He persuaded Depardieu to take the part by letting him (and his friends) 'improve' the script, which went through five drafts. Depardieu remarked that the film was 'perhaps a little light' but quite enjoyed making something that hurled flaming sociological arrows into the higher echelons of the grand bourgeoisie. Baye says it was not a 'magical' film, like *Martin Guerre*. 'Gérard was not *en forme*; he was too fat and not happy with himself.' As a lightweight film squeezed in between superproduction *Fort Saganne* and

Maurice Pialat's cop film *Police, Rive Droite-Rive Gauche* served as a pleasant staging-post for him to rest his fire, his violence and his exactitude.

The tense, dark, violent *Police*, meanwhile, was not going to be an easy film to make, even though Pialat and Depardieu had by this time bridged their personal differences. *Police* is about heroin-dealers in Paris. Depardieu plays a cop (his first time on the opposite side to the 'bad boys') who falls for a teenage drug-courier (Sophie Marceau). It is a heavily unflattering portrait of the forces of the law and he refused to prepare for his role amongst real police 'because a cop, whether you like it or not, is a piece of shit'.

Depardieu reportedly found the film depressing to make. He and Pialat drank too much, and his body blew up to 116 kilos during shooting. (This might have been due to the plot. One British critic advised that the film carry a stern warning against alcohol consumption before viewing because of the 'ferocious level of concentration required' to grasp it.) Co-star Sophie Marceau said that he was 'withdrawn and self-centred', and Sandrine

As a designer yuppie rebel in Rive Droite-Rive Gauche, *with Nathalie Baye, 1984*

His first cop role in Police, *1985, with Sophie Marceau, 1985*

Bonnaire, who had a token role, complained that he and Pialat formed a mutual-admiration society on set. In the production notes, the character of cop Mangin reads like something that might have been written as an early profile of the actor himself: 'There is something mild beneath his appearance. When you get on his nerves, he explodes and when he explodes he starts beating people up, and he doesn't like that! He's learned everything but never shot anybody. His mother didn't like him . . .' and so on.

'To a cop everybody is suspect,' comments Depardieu. 'He can bang up mother, father, child. I tried to humanise him by playing a cop who falls in love with a sixteen-year-old girl.' He took the role partly because Mangin takes the side of an immigrant. '*Police* could be shown in any major city. New York, Amsterdam, London,' he says. 'It's a story of immigrants who force their integration into a different society by any means whatsoever. It's like an Irish Catholic in a Protestant street. He's offered no means of integration, so he chooses violence. It's about some Tunisians who, in order to survive, sell and resell heroin, the same as Al Capone's Sicilians in Chicago in the 30s. It's the life I'd be leading, as a Frenchman, in another country.'

As *Police* won him the Best Actor award at the 1985 Venice Film Festival, where he was snapped laughing his head off with Danielle Mitterrand on a vaporetto trip, it is somehow unlikely that that particular fate awaits him.

15

From Drag to Disability

Somebody once said that Depardieu had a heady *je ne sais quoi* that marked him out and 'stains the memory as he leaves the room'. Whether it's his physique, which is smaller off screen than on, or his outsize character with its wild streak mixed with the naive, he is, once seen, never forgotten.

At the 1985 Cannes festival, he was there for *Fort Saganne* with co-star Deneuve. She was, as usual, the elegant iceberg, he the walking volcano in scuffed cowboy boots, a leather jacket that had seen many journeys and a T-shirt with its sleeves ripped off. As he strode down the Croisette, women either stared and swooned, or drew away in nervous unease, perhaps reiterating to themselves what producers had advised Blier when casting *Les Valseuses*. 'Do not cast Depardieu because he'll scare women.' It was during this Cannes that he casually remarked at a press conference that Deneuve was the man he'd like to be. He'd seen in her qualities he'd like to have and said so. He admired her strength, her force, her levelheadedness. Having so often played the physically strong male fascinated by his own capacity for femininity, he appears to harbour instinctively a certain ambivalence to the roles of the sexes.

'Acting is an entirely feminine profession,' he has been heard to say, 'and there's a feminine side of me. I'm much more open when I think as a woman than when I think as a man. I don't know any great film director who doesn't have a certain femininity. Men are good only for going off to war, the idiots. I prefer to stay home and do a bit of cooking.

'I've always maintained that an actor should be allowed to display that degree of femininity there is in every man, and that's why, when Bertrand Blier wanted me to go all the way in *Tenue de Soirée* and dress in women's clothing at the end, I didn't have any problems.'

Isabelle Adjani says there is 'an asexual side to Gérard'. His friendships with women are not staging-posts to a love affair but relationships to be deepened and preserved. His closeness to his co-stars is, in a way, more intimate than if they slept together. He believes in fidelity, yet relishes declaring how much he loves eating, drinking and getting laid, and, with bravado, will throw in colourful references to his private whims. More and more the message one gets from Depardieu is that whether on screen or off screen, he does what he likes. He has worked himself into a position where he can say what he feels like without being challenged and choose his work with a completely free hand. (He reportedly turns down four scripts a month.) Often he does a job because it means working with his film 'family'. If it's with an *auteur*, like Duras, he'll do it for nothing. If it's for one of the more turbulent of the *enfant terrible* directors, he'll do it for very little.

'I only ask for a lot of money when I know a film is going to be bad,' he chortles.

However, nice as the film 'family' idea might seem to be, it is sometimes the wrong idea for Depardieu, as his second film with Daniel Vigne, *Une Femme ou Deux* (*One Woman or Two*), turned out to be. The two men had worked well together on *Martin Guerre*, so *Une Femme ou Deux* seemed a natural reunion. The script was based on an idea by Vigne, and American actress Sigourney Weaver was happy to be invited to join a French film and work in French. The story required Depardieu, as a French archaeologist who has just uncovered the first Frenchwoman (a two-million year old fossil), to interact with an American foundation which wishes to link its name to the discovery and finance its research. At Charles de Gaulle airport he mistakes the leggy, lissom Sigourney Weaver (an advertising executive) for the foundation executive, played by short, elderly radio and television talk-show sexpert, Dr Ruth Westheimer.

'It's very difficult to confuse Sigourney with Dr Ruth, but I managed to do it,' said Depardieu lamely, shrugging off the embarrassingly unfunny comedy. It was a role he'd have best left unplayed. But with fifty-five films to his name by the closing days of 1985, Depardieu was determined to leave no role unplayed.

In January 1986, he made his musical comedy début on stage with one of France's icons, the dark-eyed singer-songwriter, Barbara. The 'fragile

Depardieu with his two women, Sigourney Weaver and a fossil, in Une Femme ou Deux, *1985*

black eagle' and the 'bulky blonde crook' shared top billing for *Lily Passion*, a spectacular show written by Barbara, directed by Roger Planchon and presented by leading pop impresario Albert Koski, which was premièred at the TNP in Lyons before moving it to Le Zenith, a huge modern auditorium in Paris mainly used for rock concerts. *Lily Passion* was a strange piece of theatre which told the story of a crazy killer, deeply in love with Barbara, who murders various innocent people in each town in which she sings. Barbara, a legendary exponent of the French *chanson* and Depardieu's close friend, sang, while 'the killer' Depardieu sang, prowled and declaimed poetry.

They'd taken four years to get their act together and Barbara had sent Depardieu tapes of the songs to each location where he was filming. Sometimes he'd ring her long distance and sing the songs back over the phone. Depardieu had already done variety shows with Johnny Hallyday and other buddies, but this was the real thing, the sort of spectacle that 'the little escaped vagabond from Châteauroux' loved – brave, dramatic and modern, putting your neck on the line.

More than 6,000 people nightly went wild over the couple at Le Zenith. A double album with a romantic and moody cover of them tangled in an embrace was recorded. They toured France for four sell-out months with their show, performing in hangars, gymnasiums and sports stadiums. Depardieu loved it, playing the strolling player, a troubadour. Barbara said of her co-star that he was 'an oak with the nerves of a reed'. Depardieu said, in a letter to her in his book, that her soul was a melody. Years later, they are still a cult couple and *Lily Passion* is recalled with reverence.

At roughly the same time as he was singing, Depardieu was also shooting *Tenue de Soirée* (*Evening Dress*) for Bertrand Blier, working pre-production on his role for the third outing with Richard and Veber in *Les Fugitifs* and working post-production on Claude Berri's *Jean de Florette*.

Tenue de Soirée came out four months before *Jean de Florette*. The film has an outrageous mood with Depardieu as a homosexual criminal called Bob who accosts a couple (Miou-Miou and Michel Blanc) at a dance and after a little encouragement convinces them of the thrills of theft. As reluctant burglars, blonde gold-digging Monique and wimpish, dumpy Antoine, her transvestite husband, succumb to a curious *ménage à trois*, which ends up with Bob and Antoine in full transvestite regalia tarting for trade on Paris's tawdry rue St Denis, while Monique is packed off to Spain with a personable pimp – a bizarre three-way affair even by Blier's standards.

As the Paris posters declared, it is true *putain de film*, another of Blier's super-cynical *aventures de merde* into the world of amoral and flamboyant satire. Depardieu said that what particularly appealed to him in the role was that it was like his own life, in the sense that he too is 'a traveller'.

'I've been part of all kinds of groups and gangs,' he said. 'I've met a lot of strange people in my time. I would be miserable if I wasn't able to lead this "eclectic" life; that's my form of honesty. And if one is going to get along in our society, honesty is essential.'

Tenue de Soirée was, for him, something like *Les Valseuses* projected into the year 2000. He took it on an understanding from Blier that it would be shot fast, as he was singing on stage nightly and savoured a sense of urgency.

'The film was made all round with a feeling of urgency,' says Depardieu matter-of-factly, 'the urgency for Blier to "let out" something which had long been heating up inside him, the urgency for me to carry out the stage show and the movie at the same time. That's the kind of urgency I like more and more. I believe it is the guarantee of genuineness. I get fed up

Left: In drag with Michel Blanc for Tenue de Soirée, *1986. Above: Drag comedy with Michel Piccoli in* René La Canne, *1977*

working in huge-budget films which stifle actors and everybody else. I want to get to the point and fast!'

Serge Gainsbourg wrote the music. Mylene Demongeot and Bruno Cremer also starred, and they raced through it in a month.

Once again Blier chose to show misogyny, with Miou-Miou, who in *Les Valseuses* had hardly been depicted as a romantic woman, insulted, pelted with money and relegated to a cot while Depardieu makes a play for her husband in his leopard-skin scants. Depardieu dismisses any accusations of condoning misogyny. 'When people call Blier misogynistic, that's when you know it's a word invented by machos. Women love Blier's films. They can like being treated like a scullery maid. Women can also be masochists. Just as actors have to be. The only difference is that most actors don't know they are. I do and I love it! I'm a masochist for life.'

He adds that he doesn't consider *Tenue de Soirée* to be a film about homosexuality. 'It's just about love,' he explains in the vague and un-focussed voice he employs when delving into concepts. 'To be a good actor you have to let the feminine side show. I don't mean being a fag, I mean dropping the macho side, letting the tenderness underneath come through.

Every actor was scared of taking the role of Antoine. One actor told me: "I've got to think of my fans. What would they say if you fucked me?" So I said, "Don't worry about it. We'll just rewrite it and you can fuck me!"'

The part of Antoine won Blanc the 1986 Best Actor award at Cannes, well-earned after having to go through what the average Frenchman would prefer not to have to do on screen – dress up as a woman and kiss another man under the scrutiny of the camera. Depardieu lent Blanc his Porsche to cheer him up and, with their hearts in their mouths, they got down to it.

Before Depardieu slipped into drag he had spent the best part of a year, from April to December of 1985, working with Claude Berri as the doomed hunchback on *Jean de Florette*. He arrived on the *Florette* set the day he finished *Une Femme ou Deux* and immediately slipped into his 'hump' (attached by a sort of vest) to get used to moving in an entirely different way.

'I might be playing the part of a hunchback but it is the others who are the monsters in this film,' he joked.

The film is based on the 1920s novel by French Academician Marcel Pagnol, and Depardieu as Jean, son of Florette, plays a tax collector who inherits a farm, Les Romarins, in Provence, and falls victim to an avaricious village schemer (Yves Montand) and his mentally retarded nephew, Ugolin (Daniel Auteuil), who want his land. By blocking up his only water supply, it is only a matter of time before the struggling, valiant Jean and his farming projects dry out and die.

It is a bucolic and beguiling story of innocence and evil, greed and revenge in a bygone era which Berri fought to film. He'd found a copy of *L'Eau des Collines*, Pagnol's two-volume epic, in the bookstore of the Hotel Mamounia in Marrakesh, Morocco, while taking a break from producing *Tess* in 1978. For six years, during which Berri produced a dozen films and directed three, Pagnol's widow refused to grant him the rights to the novels. Finally with the help of Alain Poiré, a producer at Gaumont Films and a close friend of the Pagnol family, Berri and Gaumont were given permission.

Next came the problem of the adaptation itself. How to put the two novels on film? And the finance – the cost of each film (requiring four seasons) would cost more than four times the cost of an average French feature, which is made for about $2 million-plus. Gaumont withdrew from

The patriarchal Papet (Yves Montand) and his victim Jean (Depardieu) in Jean de Florette, *1986*

the project. Berri's own company, Renn Productions, joined forces with three others – one of them D.D. Productions. He began by casting Montand, who had grown up in Provence and had been a friend of Marcel Pagnol, for the role of village patriarch, Le Papet. Montand took the role, of a man much older than himself, on the urging of his wife Simone Signoret.

The Ugolin role was originally destined for the enormously popular actor Coluche but at the reading Coluche (who died in a motorbike accident while the film was being shot) was unable to affect the necessary clipped Provençal accent. After being rejected by Berri on the grounds that he was too good-looking, Avignon-born Auteuil eventually got the role.

Casting Gérard Depardieu was easy, but Berri is quick to say that even if he hadn't got Gérard he would have still wanted Elisabeth Depardieu for the role of Aimée, Jean's wife. Then, seven years after he first read *L'Eau des Collines*, Berri started shooting *Jean de Florette* and *Manon des Sources*.

'Jean de Florette resembles me,' reveals Depardieu, at heart a peasant but, like Jean, from an urban background. 'It's difficult to play a character who's so similar to oneself. You don't have any perspective, you reveal yourself.'

He'd read – and cried over – Pagnol's books at the suggestion of Jean-Louis Livi, and loved the story and Pagnol's language. 'It is beautiful, this novel, this film. Everything is in it – the earth, the water, the sun and human reactions. This is film the way I imagined it as a child.'

He was less taken with Provence, which held no special allure for the actor, who prefers the north with its cold weather and less sun. 'Provence must have been beautiful when Pagnol wrote. Now it is nothing, it is mute. Like a woman who has been caressed too much, it's lost its shape.'

The pull of the film was to work again with Berri ('I didn't have a big role in *Je Vous Aime* but I'd liked Claude enormously') and with his film 'family', which included Nuytten, Montand, his friend Auteuil and, of course, his wife Elisabeth.

'I also liked the idea of a very long shoot with all the rigours that come with it. I adore long shoots, like *1900*, which took us more than a year, and *Saganne.*'

Jean with the slow but stealthy Ugolin (Daniel Auteuil)

'Provence is like a woman who has been caressed too much, it's lost its shape' –
Depardieu on location with Jean de Florette

Jean de Florette broke box-office records worldwide for a subtitled film.
In France a million people saw it in its first week of release and it went on
to out-perform top-grossing films in France like *Rambo* and *Raiders of the
Lost Ark*. An overnight classic, it sparked off a Pagnol renaissance. (Since
then, *La Gloire de Mon Père* (*My Father's Glory*) and *Le Château de Ma
Mère* (*My Mother's Castle*), produced by Gaumont with Alain Poiré as
executive producer, have been also filmed. At the Césars in 1987, *Jean de
Florette* was nominated for Best Film with *Tenue de Soirée*. Both films failed
to win. The critics in France were still snubbing Depardieu who, in turn,
called the Césars a 'joke'. Daniel Auteuil, however, won Best Actor.

Depardieu at one of his favourite pastimes, drinking wine, as Jean de Florette

In Britain the reviews were ecstatic. It was totally unheard of for a film from Europe to capture the hearts of mainstream British audiences. At the British Oscars, the BAFTA Awards, *Jean de Florette* swept the board with a dozen nominations, winning Best Film, Best Supporting Actor and Best Adapted Screenplay.

16

Blazing to Burn Out

By the end of 1986 Depardieu was falling prey to the turbulent contradictions he often played on screen. He had been burning himself into a
state of exhaustion. How long he thought he could keep it up is a matter
between him and his driven soul but signals were flashing that the time
had come to pause and reflect.

They were the red lights he least wanted to see. Staying one hundred
per cent intensely committed to acting with a workaholic's fervour possibly
meant that the inner side of his life didn't have to be confronted. Getting
to grips with life's inherent insecurities and coming to terms with any
anxieties that might have been pursuing him could be pushed aside.

Like many actors, he is a different man, at work – lighter, more carefree –
than at home. As Nathalie Baye says: 'The problem of not coping well
when you're not in work is an actor's "thing". When you work, your head
is filled from the moment the car picks you up early in the morning until
you get home late that night. There is no time for anything else.'

Depardieu once said: 'The reason I work so much is that it frees up the
feelings I have inside me that I can't express otherwise.' Indeed, his most
compelling trait is his willingness to probe the lurking emotional tremors,
exposing himself in a manner most actors wouldn't dare contemplate. 'I
think actors should do everything they want, but what counts is to express
truth. I'm passionate about my work but one can't be so protective of
one's image, only making the one film that will be the best that year.' As
he has always said, he is famous for his acting, not for how much money

141

he makes, unlike so many of his Stateside colleagues. 'I don't find it difficult to play in a film which pulls in a lot of money but that's not why I do the job.'

Yet he does, in his way, care fiercely about money. Depardieu jokes about only asking for a big fee if he knows the film is going to be a bad one, yet he hates to be slighted when it comes to payment. When cast alongside De Niro in *1900*, for instance, he was only twenty-five and largely unknown outside France. They were going to pay him about $60,000. When he learned that De Niro was getting $120,000 to play an equally lengthy role, he made a fuss, along the lines of: Hang on, we have a director (Bertolucci) who has this Communist thing, yet is going to pay the American (De Niro) more than the Frenchman (Depardieu). 'Equal status was important to me and I wanted to bring Bernardo's political sensibilities around to practical realities: the stars get paid the same.'

Depardieu got $120,000.

'I could fall flat on my face for asking too much and end up with no work at all but, shit, I could still do theatre. Or I could sing for a living!' Or simply retire on his earnings and be a full-time *vigneron*. But ambition drives him on, as it did until the end of 1986, just before he peaked – and almost expired in sheer exhaustion. He had made sixty films in fifteen years, a workload reminiscent of Hollywood in the 30s and 40s. He was depleted after the mammoth 1985 shoot on *Jean de Florette* which ended as he moved onto *Tenue de Soirée* and then the *Lily Passion* tour. As 1986 dawned he must already have been feeling the pace when he took a cameo in *Rue du Départ* (*Departure Street*), a small-budget psychodrama made by Tony Gatlif, a friend of Spanish-gypsy descent who'd also been a *voyou* and had trodden a similar path to the cinema.

'He was very keen to do it because it was the first time he would be playing the father of a teenage girl,' says Gatlif.

Then he took another tiny cameo as a prisoner in a cell in *Je Hais Les Acteurs* (*I Hate Actors*) – an 'actors' movie, indeed, made in black and white about Hollywood in the 40s. Based on Ben Hecht's novel and directed by Gérard Krawczyk, if you blink you miss Gérard.

For some time he had been preparing for another *Boy's Own* romp with his special 'team', Pierre Richard and Francis Veber, called *Les Fugitifs*. The story this time has Depardieu as a bank robber on the mend who is taken hostage by an incompetent first-time crook (Richard) and ends up on the run as one half of France's oddest couple. The physical and verbal gags between the two men are neatly offset by some often touching scenes between Lucas and the crook's young autistic daughter (Anaïs Bret). The humour is sharp, as in *Les Compères* and *La Chèvre*, and it is one of France's favourite comedies.

Pleasing as it was for Depardieu to produce something mainstream and popular, the element of moral challenge was chafing away under his skin. Pialat's powerful and controversial religious *Sous le Soleil de Satan (Under Satan's Sun)* was waiting to be made. Based on a novel written in 1926 by Georges Bernanos, a celebrated Catholic author, it deals with a country priest's confrontation with evil. For French cinema it would be the first film to touch on the inflammatory subject of aspects of spiritual and physical struggle in the faith since Robert Bresson's superb study of a young French priest, *Diary of a Country Priest*, made in 1950. Pialat's film was presented at Cannes at the 1987 festival. It won the highest award, a Golden Palm, but dissidents in the audience booed and jeered. There were those who said it was because the critics found the film static and verbose; equally likely is that beneath the jeering were generations of Catholicism woven profoundly into the fabric of the essentially European audience. Pialat, who was there to nurse his latest offspring, raised his fist to them and cried out: 'You don't like me and I don't like you.' The film's producer, Daniel Toscan du Planter, made an official statement about how the film was 'completely French, a work deeply rooted in our traditional culture' and added that it was the 'eternal story of our "captive souls", of man's divinity in the middle of his own shit and mud'. Alongside him was the atheistic Pialat, with his stubbly grey beard, ferocious gaze and often sharp tongue, being impressively vociferous in the cradle of French cinema.

Pialat had adapted the novel himself, having discovered it at the age of twenty-five when he got such a jolt that even at that time he knew he had to make it into a provocative picture. As Depardieu loves to say with a little wiggle for shock impact, *Under Satan's Sun* is a hell of an atheistic movie. He plays a young, conscience-wracked, rural priest with stooping shoulders in flowing cassock called Father Donissan. Rigidly doctrinaire, he is a strong but frustrated man who ultimately believes that Satan has conquered the world. Unafraid to fight the powers of darkness and wrestle with the devil, he knows he does so at the price of his soul, particularly when he senses the devil in the heart of Mouchette, the brewer's daughter (Sandrine Bonnaire). Pialat had consistently thought Depardieu was cut out for the Donissan character and, as the director who 'found' Bonnaire as a young teenager when casting *A Nos Amours*, had always wanted her for the

143

Mouchette role. The role of Dean Menou-Segrais, Donissan's superior, he kept for himself.

'At first I couldn't come to grips with the story of Father Donissan,' Depardieu told me after the screening, making mock-crucifix, self-whipping movements to his back. 'It was a very hard film to make but finally I delved into it and it was like a revelation.'

For him, having been brought up in a family steeped in Catholicism, the enigma of good and evil was like a punch on the nose.

'I didn't like the role but I liked the idea of playing a priest who is very stiff, stuck with himself, weighted by uncertainties and doubts about his belief.

'I'd rather believe in God or a "good spirit" than in evil. But certainly I don't know how to explain the would-be "existence" of God. I am not at ease with such "big matters".

'Catholicism is very strange, because it's a religion that forgives, that absolves. But it's also twisted, with its Seven Deadly Sins and all that.' Patently he derives some joy from doing films which could be considered almost 'sinful', overstepping the mark and riding against tradition in an

Depardieu and Sandrine Bonnaire at Cannes Film Festival 1987 for Sous le Soleil de Satan

144

As Abbé Donissan in Sous le Soleil de Satan

essentially Catholic-based society. 'I became a Muslim for two years, from fifteen to seventeen. I thought it was a beautiful religion. It lets you talk to God casually.' He dropped Islam for Elisabeth, whom he had just met. She suggested it wasn't really working for him. 'She was absolutely right.' It was the wrong protection device for his survival technique.

At the Césars, *Sous le Soleil* brought him, once again, a nomination. (Richard Bohringer won it for *Le Grand Chemin.*) Although he had said nothing publicly about being nominated ten times and winning it only once (for *Le Dernier Métro* – 'I have no desire to be judged by members of this profession,' he commented), word trickled out that he was tired, hurt and probably furious. Although he had the standard 'no comment' to make on the subject, he knew the point had come to cool off.

145

He refused to commit himself to anything apart from promising to play Rodin in *Camille Claudel* for Isabelle Adjani, whose project it was. He said he would do it if she would wait for him to drop out for a while 'to think things over'. Freedom, he said, should be savoured like 'a good cup of tea'. He went on his tea break.

On and off for five months he and Elisabeth toured the Middle East and Latin America, and Depardieu spent some of his sabbatical representing one film or another at festivals abroad. Moscow won't forget in a hurry his presence at the film festival there when, in the bar of the Rossiya Hotel, amidst an international throng of cineasts, the bulky Frenchman threw up after his umpteenth vodka. Possibly it was the thought of finding the way back to his room in the 6,000-sleeper hotel, which David Robinson, film critic of the London *Times*, compared to being as challenging geographically as 'Dartmoor without a map'.

He was also invited by London's National Film Theatre to do a live question-and-answer *Guardian* Lecture on stage on the final night of their season of fifteen of his films. He accepted happily, Britain being a country he favoured for its puddings. And for its film-making. Albert Finney's *Tom Jones* had made a lasting impression on him as a youth; John Gielgud, Laurence Olivier and Ralph Richardson were of course his British 'greats'.

Accompanied by his friend, producer René Cleitman, he stayed at The Savoy in the same riverside suite used by one of his heroes, director Martin Scorsese. Confronting an English audience live for the first time was clearly nerve-wracking and he apparently sought Dutch courage in several drinks beforehand. Derek Elley, who chaired the event, recalls Depardieu being very relaxed about it all until he actually was on stage.

'Live audiences do strange things to film people,' says Elley. 'From where I was sitting I could see a sweat break out on his brow, but he didn't seize up like so many actors and directors do. As he warmed to his subject, he started to play to the audience, putting on a bit of a show, giving them plenty of banter and chatting up the interpreter sitting between us. He was slightly overdoing it, because he was a bit nervous.

'He worked the room and had a lot of fun with some puns. The one that brought the biggest laugh was when I asked him about working with a group – *une bande* – of film friends which ultimately became all about film-making being one huge erection – *"bander"* being slang for having a hard-on – and the cinema being a "beautiful prostitute".'

The interpreter recalls being totally thrown by the radical way in which his behaviour changed once he was actually on stage.

'I had interpreted at his press interviews during the couple of days of his visit,' she recounts. 'His calm, polite, unhurried and highly articulate manner of conducting these interviews was every interpreter's dream.

'Within seconds of being on stage, I could hardly believe that I was interpreting for the same man! He completed only some of his sentences, darting from topic to topic, would stop halfway through a sentence or anecdote because he couldn't remember why he was telling it and on more than one occasion he greeted my translation with the French equivalent of "Are you sure you got that right?"

'During the press interviews he had treated me formally and with a certain degree of professional respect. Once on stage, however, he adopted an attitude of implied intimacy, clearly wanting to give the audience the impression that there was "a little something" going on between us.

'It turned into an interpreter's nightmare. But the audience loved his whole performance and the more outrageous he became the more they loved it – Depardieu was giving them exactly what they wanted and had come for.'

The *Guardian* Lecture offered few insights but afterwards, over dinner at Soho's Groucho Club and in the taxi back to his hotel, he'd drop casual remarks about his wine cellar being stocked with 7,000 bottles and how he liked to slaughter a pig for the table.

The Depardieus spent most of that summer at their Normandy house, a villa in Trouville, two hours north of Paris. Trouville is a pleasantly *recherché* resort in the shadow of Deauville and near Cabourg, Proust's Balbec. It is an old-fashioned town with madly turreted villas, cafés with red-checked gingham table cloths, faded hotels and stalls selling fish.

In the lost domain of the sands are the memories of the Normandy invasions and last season's forgotten buckets and spades. The area has been celebrated by generations of painters and writers, and Marguerite Duras has a villa nearby. When he's there he sits watching the family at play in the pool, smoking Gitanes, reading Shakespeare, Dostoevsky or de Musset, scouting for the best *calvados*, the potent apple brandy of Normandy. He might kill the fatted lamb for Sunday lunch or invite friends over and cook duck, fish, or rabbit, garnished with a simple sauce. On a good day they might be entertained by outrageously vulgar stories, which he'll tell with his lusty Rabelaisian laugh so rich you can almost taste it. On a bad day, they'd simply get the best of his wine cellar to savour.

In *Lettres Volées* he writes of his pleasure at being there alone with Elisabeth, in the tranquillity of Normandy, where they can still recapture their first moments. He loves the North with its grey skies and cool days, feeling at ease with the isolation, trees and beaches there where the sun is 'cold, almost covered by a layer of thin ice'. The cold weather, he says, makes you react.

His favourite place is where there's shade, so that like a plant, a hydrangea or a wild cyclamen, he can grow and bloom. 'My life is like my acting – a secret garden where I can give birth to things that would otherwise remain in the shade.'

Depardieu stayed away from the fire only six months before he was back, kindling the embers and blowing on the flames. He announced enthusiastically that he'd come back to take sculpture lessons for his role as Rodin in *Camille Claudel*.

17

Grand Cru on a Big Bender

After his break Depardieu said he felt as if he was boiling.

'I'm like wine,' he told Joan Dupont in an interview at Bougival for the *New York Times* magazine. 'I have good years and bad years. Now I'm a *grand cru* [a vintage wine].'

In these vintage years indeed, he was ready to let himself mellow into full-bodied claret as Auguste Rodin, the great sculptor. In keeping with his feeling that the actor is a tool and needing to be the right tool for the job, Depardieu spent several weeks attending sculpture courses at the Paris Ecole des Beaux Arts to get a sense of clay and plaster. Isabelle Adjani went to the classes with him. While she was up to her elbows in clay, he learnt how to place his hands and hold the tools. His efforts paid off. On film, working the earth and clay with prowling energy, resembling slightly a flamboyant Vincent Van Gogh, bearded with his hair short and reddish, Depardieu looks as though he's finally found paradise as a sculptor who thinks with his hands.

Camille Claudel is the story of the nineteenth-century poet Paul Claudel's sister Camille, Rodin's mistress and muse, and a sculptor in her own right, who spent her last thirty years, ignored by all, in an asylum. Rodin, a married man twenty-two years her senior, met her when she was twenty-two and invited her to Paris to be his apprentice and passion. The first kiss between Rodin and Camille (Depardieu and Adjani) hidden behind a door in the sculptor's country house while his wife and Camille's parents are dining outside in the garden is one of the screen's great moments of pure, pristine passion.

The complex tutor–pupil relationship, artistic rivalry and jealousy interfered with the lives of the two sculptors, and Camille finally came to the difficult decision that she must leave Rodin in order to fulfil herself creatively. But in losing Rodin, she lost everything and spiralled downwards into the depths of depression and mental disorder.

'Rodin was a petty-minded coward,' says Depardieu. 'Head over heels in love with Camille for five years, but as soon as she went crazy, he was off. That's what the film is about, an enormous and insane love affair – two fantastic, tortured characters.'

He wasn't familiar with Rodin when he was offered the job and accepted it because it was a true story. Then he read several biographies of the sculptor – which scarcely mentioned Camille – and was intrigued by the opportunity to examine the dynamic of male–female relationships in the nineteenth century. His Rodin is fatally attractive, an unpleasant womaniser who can't keep his hands off the clay or his nude female models.

The film was a project Adjani had nursed from concept to birth. She battled with the Claudel family for the rights and furnished a great chunk of money to make it. She also combined closely with Bruno Nuytten, the father of her son, who directs. They would have waited years to get

As Rodin in Camille Claudel, *1988*

As Rodin in Camille Claudel: *'Can't keep his hands off the clay'.*

Depardieu to do the role. 'He is the only actor whose virility and massive presence could match that of Rodin,' says Adjani. 'It is so easy to work with him. He's a man who has become so refined, so tender, over the years. He's very literary and we discussed everything. He's both masculine and feminine – a hermaphrodite, as is any good actor or actress.'

Of Adjani, a star who equals him in volatility, Depardieu says: 'Her strength of will is unbelievable. She wanted to play Camille Claudel, so she went out and got the whole thing together! A film isn't an easy thing to produce. It's difficult to think the whole thing through. You have to start by getting two or three people together – she had Bruno and me – and then you go wild. You've got to make everything explode. I don't have the patience but I can spot the craziness in people and help them take off.'

Camille Claudel won Adjani a 1989 César and Berlin Film Festival's Golden Bear for Best Actress, which countered the French press's *Prix Citron* ('Acid Overtones') awarded her some years before for her known general lack of co-operation in interviews. The film also was nominated for the 1990 Best Foreign Film award at the Oscars and won the Best Film, Cinematography, Set Design and Costumes Césars. Depardieu, who was also co-producer on the film, was nominated at the Césars for Best Actor but for the twelfth time did not win. (Jean-Paul Belmondo did, for Claude Lelouch's *Itinéraire d'un Enfant Gaté* (*Itinerary of a Spoilt Child*)).

The decade that elapsed between his winning a César for *Le Dernier Métro* in 1981 and *Cyrano* in 1991 might have been seen, in that he was noticeably overlooked, as a case of deliberate shunning by the establishment. This might have had something to do with Depardieu's pejorative remarks made publicly over the years about his peers in French film-making. Joan Dupont recounts in a *New York Times* interview being with him and Pialat when Pialat jeered at 'the New York snobs who line up to see films by Rohmer and Godard', to which Depardieu exclaimed, 'Zero! Rohmer is nothing!' When Agnès Varda, director of the extraordinary *Vagabonde*, was cited, she too was relegated to the 'snob' category; Chabrol is considered 'boring'. Depardieu told *Time Out*'s Brian Case that because he likes to participate, he's wary of directors like Claude Lelouch 'who tells his cast conflicting versions of what he wants'.

In the American magazine *Interview*, Depardieu talked about the 'big problem' being caused in France because 'the new generation of directors can't even write a decent script'. 'Luc Besson's *The Big Blue* was a catastrophe, with that stupid diving sequence,' he told journalist Stephen O'Shea. 'Then there's [Jean-Jacques] Beineix and his *Betty Blue* – that was worth watching for about five minutes.

'French cinema is in such a bad way because there are no great films being made. Of the 140 films that are made in France every year, maybe four or five are exportable. The rest are crap. And then there's another problem: there are no good young actors. French actors are stuck on themselves. They have a sort of egomania that's even worse than the one over here [USA].'

Depardieu finished his tirade on his juniors in scatalogical terms – scatology and Depardieu being no strangers – remarking that 'they strain for hours to shit a tiny turd'. 'What ever happened,' he asks with an earthy chuckle, 'to the great shits of yesteryear?'

His abrasive opinions might hold some truth but his forthrightness can hardly endear him to those who work in the same world. Yet without him there wouldn't be the French film industry there is today. His name on a film guarantees good international and French box-office returns in a climate that since the mid-1980s has seen French attendances fall from 172 million in 1985 to 135 million in 1987. Almost half his films have been distributed abroad. But then Depardieu had earned the right to have his say. In 1988, he turned forty, the age at which many lesser men like to believe they have built up enough confidence to be able to say what they think. It was also the age, he says in his tentative way, when he found childhood. 'Between twenty and thirty you are still romantic. Between thirty and forty you try to find rebirth.'

1988 was a year of changes for Depardieu. A walking parody of French elegance with his equatorial waistline and shoulder-shrugging *élan*, he was still a man of gigantic contradictions charging through life. But he was also a force to be reckoned with at the highest level. The same year his friend, François Mitterrand, was re-elected president with a second seven-year term. It was the year Depardieu's book of letters was published and two filmographic biographies, both called *Gérard Depardieu*, one by Olivier Dazat, the other by Georges Cohen, came out. Best of all, on 15 September the Ministry of Culture gave him La Croix de Chevalière (first class) at a ceremony at the Elysée Palace. His family was there as well as friend and neighbouring winemaker, Jean Jarry. The occasion overwhelmed him with pride – and with sadness, for on the night of his honour his father, Dédé died.

'On his hospital bed he looked like somebody who can't get over the fact that he was dead. His mouth was open. I'm a pretty strong guy but I had a hell of a job to close it. He took his wide-open mouth to heaven with him. He had so many things to say to his wife. He'd had plenty of time to think about it in the six months since she'd died,' writes Depardieu in *Lettres Volées*. Le Dédé died before he got to see his son's letter to him, as La Lilette had.

'About a week before she died I wanted to write to her because I never had,' the actor said regretfully. 'But I never gave the letters to her. And I just kept writing. Then my father died too – followed her.'

The loss of his parents affected Depardieu deeply. He missed them being there, in the present, their ways, their smell, the 'tick tock of their clock'. He had for years sent them money to help out and seemed to have understood well what it was that ailed them during his Châteauroux years. 'You made six children together because you were incapable of finding any other way to say "I love you",' he writes.

After *Camille Claudel*, he went straight on to a project inspired (partially) by Catherine Deneuve, joining her as a co-star and co-producer on *Drôle d'Endroit pour une Rencontre* (*A Strange Place to Meet*), a two-hander for two people whose lives overlap one winter's weekend at a roadside car park. Abandoned by her exasperated husband at a lay-by after an argument, France (Deneuve) meets Charles (Depardieu), a misanthropic surgeon,

On the autoroute with Deneuve in Drôle d'Endroit pour une Rencontre, *1988*

who is taking his broken motorcar to pieces. He wants to be alone but she petulantly refuses to leave.

Directed by a first-timer to features, François Dupeyron, it is, in the true sense of the word, a minimal road movie which was lavishly praised in France but never took off in Britain. Nigella Lawson said it all in her review in the *Sunday Times*. 'Depardieu has such lines as: "Loving someone always ends up as a kind of death," and Deneuve has to contend with the likes of: "I only want him to say he loves me." "You're mad," he says to her at one point. "Yes, I know." And that, apart from a breathless hymn in praise of the beauty of the training shoe, a number of shots of the moon disappearing into the clouds, a lot of lip trembling and staring at monkey wrenches, is that.'

When I talked to Deneuve about the film, which many feel is patently obscure, she was full of enthusiasm.

'It was the most physically challenging film I've done as it was shot almost entirely at night in winter. And I was so pleased to work with Gérard again. He is wonderful to work with. He is a very generous actor and he really likes women. That's very special in an actor: normally they are so narcissistic they only like themselves.'

154

Depardieu was vaguely ambivalent about it, saying that it was one of the films he'd made that people didn't like but he did. Another of those films was his next, a pot-boiling romance he co-produced called *Deux* (*Two*), directed by friend Claude Zidi and co-starring ageing *fille fatale* Maruschka Detmers, who is described in Jean Tulard's *Dictionnaire du Cinéma* as 'introduced by Godard in *Prénom: Carmen* [*First name: Carmen*], she was a sensation in *Le Diable au Corps* in a fellatio scene'.

With *lèvres pulpeuses* (pouting lips), she plays an estate agent who shows more than houses to Depardieu, a blond, dashing and handsome concert organiser with a hairy chest and an intense stare. Although the electricity between them is non-existent, *Deux* must have had something to it: the Americans bought the rights to make their own version. Depardieu then made another film with Alain Resnais, called *I Want To Go Home*. Based on a Jules Feiffer script, he made it in halting English ('I didn't know what I was saying half the time') and plays a Parisian caught up with an American cartoonist, played by Adolph Green.

'It's about the difference between the French and the Americans,' he explains. 'The French always have excuses for all the terrible things they do, and the Americans feel guilty all the time,' he said. Colleagues say that

Depardieu checks his lines

he did it blind because he gets a kick out of working with serious directors and loves the *cachet* he gets from it. He had not worked with Resnais since *Mon Oncle d'Amérique* in 1980. The film received a mention for its scenario at the Venice Film Festival but was universally trashed and disappeared without trace.

Between the two came *Trop Belle Pour Toi* (*Too Beautiful For You*). It was the fifth from the Blier/Depardieu stable. A thoroughly offensive comedy of manners about the complexities of a marriage breakdown, it turns our perception of beauty on its head. It is about a successful car salesman with a mid-life crisis who is married to an elegant young bourgeoise (Carole Bouquet) but in love with his middle-aged secretary (Josiane Balasko, his co-star years back in *Dîtes-Lui que Je l'Aime*), a cosy lady in a blue Terylene anorak. It is a blackly romantic triangle with a kick like a mule. The balding, bearded Blier (almost the epitome of bourgeois conformism), discussing the film in London, called it '*un film grave* but with humour'. Depardieu called it 'the story of a man who's wrecked by happiness'. Blier thought it 'gentle' while Depardieu considered it 'absolutely terrifying'.

'Generally I dislike gentle movies: cinema has an alarming tendency to be soft-centred because it's a consumer product,' said Blier. 'This one is a subversive representation of life, not a morality play. I suppose it poses a series of questions about man's weaknesses, about love considered as an illness.'

He wrote it, naturally, for Depardieu and once again drew out of the actor a performance of touching vulnerability.

'When I write a film that isn't for him,' Blier says, puffing heavily on his pipe, 'he tends to sulk. He comes sniffing round and says, "Are you sure this is going to work?" He likes the feeling of belonging.' Jean Carmet tells a story of how, when filming once, Depardieu returned to the hotel late at night and found his door locked. 'He broke it down. He hates to be shut out of anything.'

Trop Belle was the most successful film in France that year, winning the Jury's Special Grand Prix at Cannes 1989 and the Best Film at the 1990 Césars. Depardieu, again, was only nominated. (Philippe Noiret won for *La Vie et Rien D'Autre* directed by Bertrand Tavernier.)

Carole Bouquet, the actress who replaced Deneuve as The Face of Chanel, received the Best Actress award at the Césars. 'When I work with Gérard I think I'm a better actress than when I don't, which gives me a problem working with somebody else,' laughed Bouquet. 'I believe that if

At Cannes, 1989, for Trop Belle Pour Toi

you mix with stupid people you become like them – if you're with talented people you become talented. He leads, takes me away and I go.'

It was at the 1989 Cannes festival that I nearly got run over crossing the pavement-to-pavement, fan-lined Croisette by the big guy on a tiny motorbike. Depardieu, on a little buzzer loaned him by his journalist ally, Marc Esposito (editor of *Studio* and former leading light of *Première*, both of them France's top cinema magazines), was there to tubthump *Trop Belle*. American actor Nick Nolte was there to do the same for *New York Stories*.

The Depardieu/Nolte connection is worth noting. Apart from the fact they look alike – both shambling blonds, broad of beam with solid features, and an unexpected spark and delicacy – they are, according to Depardieu, very similar in character: wild boys with courteous manners.

'He played the *voyou* in *Down and Out in Beverly Hills* which was, in France, called *Boudu Sauvé des Eaux* and was my first stage play,' says the Frenchman. 'I was Boudu.' Nolte played the Depardieu role in *The Fugitives*. Although the film bombed in America, Nolte happily says that he liked the film. 'I've almost never taken on a script I thought wouldn't make a good movie,' says Nolte with a Depardieu-like sanguineness.

The story goes that Depardieu challenged Nolte to muster for a drinking contest in his room at the dignified Carlton Hotel. Inevitably Depardieu won. The two men were reported to be seen dancing together nude in the foyer of the hotel at 4 am. A correspondent from Scandinavia averred that that part of the story was wrong; according to him, they had in fact been seen mooning their bare bottoms out of the sculpted windows of the Carlton as the sun was rising. Whichever is true (possibly both), they're ripe tales, the sort of thing everyone goes to Cannes for.

18

Château and Cyrano

The British Film Institute officially doffed its cap to Depardieu on 15 October 1989, when it gave him a Fellowship for his efforts in advancing the world of film. Joining the distinguished ranks of the BFI Fellows came as an unexpected surprise. The other winner that year was Dame Peggy Ashcroft, an actress Depardieu considered a living legend. BFI Fellows include another of his heroes, Orson Welles, who once planned to direct a *Cyrano de Bergerac* screenplay, and Indian director Satyajit Ray, with whom D.D. Productions was about to get involved on a film project.

Depardieu, although he says he hates the hooliganism and alcohol abuse in Britain, has always been a bit of an Anglophile – 'English actors are geniuses on stage' – having done plays in Paris by Edward Bond, David Storey and Terence Frisby, and enjoyed many English TV series like *Fawlty Towers* and *The Jewel in the Crown*. He was also about to start a working relationship with Kenneth Branagh on *Henry V* for which he secured the French television rights. Although he didn't think the French would truly appreciate bluff Hal, French television being 'lousy' (as opposed to British television which is, in his opinion, 'admirable'), he was enormously amused to dub Branagh's soundtrack into French, especially as the play celebrates an English victory over the French army at the Battle of Agincourt.

In Branagh Depardieu found another 'brother', with 'the force and youth of an actor who's a bit like an early Orson Welles'. They talk about producing Shakespeare together, taking the classics and turning them into popular subjects. 'Gérard is a natural Othello or Anthony,' comments

Branagh. 'Part of what equips him for this, aside from a sexually charismatic presence, is his humour. He is a great actor partly because there is the most delicious twinkle in his eye. His performances are marked with great *truth*.'

So the BFI award was timely, even though awards tend to embarrass him. 'The best award, the best compensation is getting to travel around the world with a film to a festival or to promote it,' he says with delight, like a kid on a free ride. 'I'm not in this business to win prizes. I'm one of those people who is better at giving than receiving.' The BFI Fellowship was the start of a harvest of international awards which Depardieu would reap from *Cyrano de Bergerac*.

Cyrano was a film he plunged into, 'trusting his nose', for most of 1989. To take on a nineteenth-century play couched in 1,400 lines of alexandrine couplets posed a challenge of a different order. Cyrano was a character Depardieu had secretly loved all his life and dreamed of playing. He had seen an earlier film version of it once, a few years before, starring Jacques Weber, who in Rappeneau's film plays the Comte de Guiche.

'I have a big nose too, so that was a good sign,' he laughs. 'Cyrano and I, we smell life!'

Edmond Rostand's play about a valiant, long-nosed, seventeenth-century poet, braggart and swordsman, was first filmed in 1950 starring José Ferrer in a turned-up nose. It was shot in black and white with Michael Gordon directing and won Ferrer the Oscar. (Ferrer coincidentally presented Depardieu with a D.W. Griffith film award for *Cyrano* years later in 1990 in New York.) Steve Martin updated the story and donned a preposterous proboscis in his attempt to woo Daryl Hannah in *Roxanne*. (One American exhibitor of Rappeneau's *Cyrano* actually rang the film's distributor in New York and said: 'The French have done a wonderful remake of Steve Martin's *Roxanne*. It's a good story.')

Since its conception in 1897, seven film and countless TV versions have rolled through of the epic about the man with the big nose who lives and dies for the love of his cousin Roxane, who is in love with the handsome but dumb Christian. When the film rights came back into the public domain in the mid-80s, director Jean-Paul Rappeneau was asked by a group of producers if he would be interested in it. He hesitated. He hadn't seen the play since he was a child and knew that a workable screen draft needed to be done before it could even be considered. He also knew it would cost a fortune.

Two years and five drafts later, with Depardieu pencilled in for the leading role, he had something to work on. The next step was to raise the

Cyrano, as usual, behind Christian (Vincent Perez) in the race for Roxane

100 million francs needed for the venture, which had 2,000 actors and extras (mainly Hungarians doing it as a second job), forty sets inspired by Rembrandt and Vermeer, 2,000 costumes, a genuine arsenal, a man-made forest, a widened river, and lengthy location shooting in Hungary and France – and a daily fake nose for Depardieu plus all those alexandrine couplets, subtitled in English by Anthony Burgess. Depardieu, with his masterful blend of strength and vulnerability, was tailor-made for the part, born to play it both physically and spiritually.

'Cyrano is a great fighter, but a great romantic. All romantics are really children who have never grown up,' comments the self-confessed love-addict, before adding a typical Depardieu extra: 'He is a thug who wants to say "I love you". In Cyrano, you can recognise something in yourself, asking questions about life that are not so easy to find the answers to. He is a typical adolescent character, struggling with life and the feelings we all had then – not loving ourselves, thinking nobody will ever love us. Like me, he felt more comfortable with words than with looks.

'After playing him I realised he was someone who resembled me more than I thought. I feel so like Cyrano, with his courage and his fragility. He taught me much about myself, about my acting. Before, I was a little arrogant, a bit of an amateur.'

In baggy trousers and clumping boots, he can still fence like Errol Flynn and woo with the virility of a young Brando, while uttering with panache couplets of poetry so complex only a razor-sharp mind could cope with them.

Rappeneau never considered anyone but Depardieu for the role. 'From the beginning he was the only possibility, because he is the only one in France who has this blend of strength and weakness, and who is prepared to show, to act out, his feminine side.

'But perhaps the real reason that I chose him was his voice. I remembered the two films he made with Truffaut, *La Femme d'à Côté* and *Le Dernier Métro*, where he played such gentle, sad characters, with such soft voices. In Cyrano he can speak in his loud voice and in his gentle voice.'

Depardieu's Cyrano prompted instant media coverage on the ethics of beauty and the beast. The 'Big is Beautiful' debate raged. Large men started billing themselves as 'Depardieu Style' in magazine Lonely Hearts columns as years before bald men had described themselves as Kojak lookalikes. But although Depardieu tends to shrug off his weight, his brute physique has haunted him from the age of thirteen. 'I just can't seem to get on with the way I look,' he comments. 'The only thing I'm happy with is my nature – joyous, optimistic, quite fresh!'

As in *Jean de Florette*, his shape fluctuated when he was off on other projects; his weight was a problem and had, apparently, to be masked at times. 'When he is over-eating, he can be perfectly repulsive looking,' says his producer-partner and agent, Jean-Louis Livi.

'I'm not a maniac about my image,' Depardieu says with a giggle, puffing the eternal cigarette. 'But I'd rather not see mirrors. There are actually very few moments when I *really* feel good about myself.' He flexes solid pectorals over wrestlers' shoulders, smiling angelically. 'I don't want to be too hard on myself. I hate my size but then I also hate anger and injustice but I still have them within me.'

Anne Brochet, who plays the beautiful, tiny Roxane, found working with Depardieu and what she calls 'his animal instincts' daunting at first.

'Gérard is very disturbing,' she said after the film was finished. 'The mixture of brutality and refinement is very strange. He was so surprising. He can't be happy if the person in front of him is not happy. You have to be very simple, honest. He wants to see a true reaction. As soon as you start to bluff or fake he feels it. Happily we found as certain harmony, even in the way our voices came together.'

162

As Cyrano with Roxane (Anne Brochet), 1990

If Rappaneau intended to make it a *Cyrano* for the Rocky generation he succeeded brilliantly. The man who is the French population's favourite literary character has had a field day. As a subtitled film, it hit highest ever takings worldwide. As a prize winner it took, among others, America's Golden Globe for Best Foreign Film, various Césars after an unprecedented thirteen nominations, and was nominated for an Oscar (Best Foreign Film). It even made Paris' toughest film critics break into applause. At the same screening, Catherine Deneuve burst into tears.

The film opened in Paris in March 1990, barely six weeks after Belmondo – in latex nostrils – had opened, to rave reviews, in a mega-stage production of *Cyrano* at the Théâtre Marigny for Robert Hossein. They were both superb and the battle of prominent probosces was immediately dubbed France's War of the Noses. The duel of nasal attractions almost burst into flames when *Elle* magazine ran a caricature which, according to Belmondo's lawyer, showed Belmondo with Depardieu 'as if he [Depardieu] were the real Cyrano and Belmondo was just a poor little guy'. The court took Belmondo's side but awarded him only one franc. Belmondo laughed it off, tossing his nose, at the end of one performance, into the audience as they leaped from their seats to applaud.

Depardieu also laughed. In reality the two leading men of different generations had equal billing and were both fabulously successful.

'I'm suspicious of success,' Depardieu said. 'I'm a bit of a peasant about it. You need four seasons to know what's going on. There are good harvests and bad harvests. Success is like growing grapes. I prefer to believe in talent.'

Depardieu's harvest philosophy serves him well. When not reaping awards, he is picking grapes during the *vendange* (grape harvest) at the splendid fourteenth-century château near Angers that he bought in the late 80s. His vineyards already produce four different Anjou wines, the most select being *Cuvée Cyrano*. Depardieu's Château de Tigné is in gentle countryside which reflects a rich past. It's a grandiose stone building with a gravel courtyard, complete with hilltop tower, mullioned windows and castellated turrets, skirted by a fast-flowing river and surrounded by twenty-five hectares (about sixty acres) of immaculate vineyards. He bought it by 'instinct rather than choice'.

It stands a stone's throw from Tigné, a small village that peaks in a grey-stone church spire which overlooks a cluster of square, red-roofed houses. The château itself doesn't interest the owner half as much as the vineyards. From the rough-hewn stone tower, he can survey his territory as *châtelain* and imagine he's living six centuries ago.

'The most beautiful thing to own in the world is land,' he says. 'I'm too rooted to the land to understand the city. The land clears the head.'

The château is close enough to Bougival for him to be able to reach it if only for the day and whenever he can Depardieu heads to Tigné to roll up his sleeves and work on the wine-making process with his team of men. It has ostensibly replaced the holidays he took when he got bored.

'Here I try and never get bored. I expect Elisabeth and the children get a bit fed up.' Wine is, in his words, his joy in life, its essence 'the Mozart of the mouth'. He says he can recognise a wine like he recognises a friend. 'I would rather not drink than drink a bad wine. My wine is like me – not *à la mode*. Real wine. Strong. Natural. No sugar.' He could add 'robust' and 'versatile'.

At Tigné they produce 60,000 bottles a year. He also has half a hectare in Burgundy producing Nuits St Georges. Wine-making has become Depardieu's consuming passion. In his passport, on the page opposite the one that says Gérard Xavier Depardieu, his occupation is given as '*Acteur-Vigneron*' – Actor-Winemaker – and he has been known to leave a film shoot to check the progress of his harvest.

Vigneron *Depardieu tends his grapes*

His new ambition, he purrs like a contented cat with newly spruced whiskers, is to help the wine of Anjou be recognised one day as great wine. Not necessarily *his* wine – all Anjou wine. At the modest end of the wine scale, it is not, as he says, Château-Lafite. The region mainly produces country rosé, which a few years ago moved into a new era when rosé was renamed 'blush' and gained a certain respectability. There are also dry whites and spicy red cabernets. Cabernet is Depardieu's favourite. He likes 'well-made wines that don't taste of the wood, even when they are a bit young and still fairly rough on the tongue. And they must not have too ostentatious a nose!

'I told my cellar-master that I don't want *Cuvée Cyrano* to have a bouquet. It is appropriate in that Cyrano hates people to notice his nose but the current fashion is for wine with very flamboyantly developed aromas, like actor's egos. I want a wine that doesn't bombard you with an aroma, but is more subtle. Like acting, it shouldn't be overdone.'

In a Depardieu-worshipping but revealing documentary called *Gérard Depardieu: Vigneron*, made in 1990 by France's Canal Plus, the apprenticeship he served as an adolescent labourer in the vineyards of Burgundy and the Côtes-du-Rhône, is shown as well rewarded. With unveiled glee and joy, he prunes vines, picks grapes, drives the tractor, discusses matters with his estate manager, Dominique, strides among the fermentation vats and wooden barrels in vaulted cellars, tasting, swilling and smelling his wine, checking sediment, testing temperatures, noting alcohol content and letting his taste buds savour the body. The ritual, if it warrants it, is completed without spitting out but swallowing the liquid in an appreciative gulp. Depardieu taps his nose knowingly. 'This is very useful as it is good for smelling the true bouquet.' Watching him work in muddy boots and brown hat with his new-found 'wine family' – similar to the way he mixes with his 'film family' – it is almost as if the prodigal son has finally returned to his *real* home.

With his father-figure friend Jean Carmet, another man who appears to have the constitution of a bull, he goes to the village bistro Le Caméleon to join the locals in a wine tasting. They organise a return bout at the château, in the barn lined with firewood where a suckling pig turns on the spit and the farm dogs gnaw bones in the foreground. Perhaps the high point of the film is when Depardieu flies in from New York, having taken leave from the making of *Green Card*, and returns to Tigné for the village's annual wine-making festival. There, in the first rays of spring sunshine, he

Depardieu at home with his own cuvée *at Château de Tigné, in Anjou*

drinks and chats and plunges his nose into endless glasses, while Carmet conducts a little orchestra of musicians in red waistcoats and boaters playing traditional tunes; the locals, dressed in artisan gear, dance in the village square.

Some of Canal Plus's film was included in a Channel Four documentary on Depardieu with the ungainly but appropriate title of *The Ugly Frog That Became a Prince*. Transmitted in Britain in March 1991, mere days after the storm broke in America about his 'admission' of childhood rapes, it was even more revealing than Canal Plus's. Interviewed by his friend, Michel Denisot, the day after he'd flown by Concorde from America, he was patently tired and tense from recent events, yet was trusting enough to say what he felt. When asked when he felt most relaxed in life, he replied: 'In a wine cellar with friends and in bed with a woman.'

The latter, in French, is an abstract concept. It is understood that one is talking about the allegory of love and affection, and not extra-marital sexual liaisons. He pauses on screen, looking awkward, before expanding his meaning, which is to be in bed 'next to someone with whom you can recall the past, relive things together, draw things out of each other, harmony' – in short, the ideal of romance. But once again, the way he puts it is almost too frank, too intimate, for public consumption.

There has never been anybody around him, any of his henchmen in the entourage, who vets his stuff, as a Hollywood publicist would, tells him to temper his disarming honesty under the merciless scrutiny of the media. Sometimes certain things should not be told. If he'd been a little more cautious in his public relations he probably would have won the Oscar for Best Actor for *Cyrano* at the 1991 awards.

But soon after he was nominated 'L'Affaire Depardieu' was to break.

19

America: Are they Real or is the Jacket Padded?

The Australian director Peter Weir, after directing *The Mosquito Coast* in 1986, wanted to return to writing. Since his success with *Picnic at Hanging Rock*, he'd spent a long time working away from home, with Mel Gibson and *The Year of Living Dangerously* and Harrison Ford and *Witness*. It was time to go to Australia to mull things over.

One day in Sydney he saw, for the second time, Andrzej Wajda's *Danton*. He was again so struck by Depardieu's performance that his wife, the production designer Wendy Stites, suggested that he adapt a short story he had written in 1983 about a 'green-card' marriage into a script for the Frenchman. Weir pulled the manuscript out of a bottom drawer in his desk, cut out a picture of Depardieu from his local newspaper, stuck it above his typewriter and began writing. He wanted to tell Depardieu, who was then in Australia, but didn't. Ironically, Depardieu at the time was telling people how much he admired the work of Peter Weir.

'When I wrote the film my idea was to have an English actor in the lead,' explains Weir. 'The story is in the mould of *It Happened One Night* with an American marrying a foreigner (Clark Gable and Claudette Colbert) for mutual convenience. I had been looking for the right actor, somebody with a Cary Grant or Spencer Tracy range, but was alarmed to discover that the necessary non-threatening sex appeal and screen charm needed for the role seemed to have evaporated. I could find no English actor capable of carrying the picture.'

By the time he finished the script he knew that no one else could be his leading man but Depardieu, who was thrilled to receive a script from 'the other side of the world'.

'I was very surprised that Peter Weir would write a film just for me,' blusters Depardieu with a windmill of hand gestures. 'I was also pleased that he was *un auteur*. I much prefer to work with the author of the piece. I follow the author. I always try to follow good friends who can tell a good story. I had always liked the way Peter handled love scenes, making them just one kiss after a long seduction. Just like Truffaut. No nudity, just great sexual tension.'

Weir went to France to meet him and the two men got on famously. But Depardieu had four films lined up back-to-back and wouldn't be free for ages. He went off to make *Cyrano*, Weir went off to direct *Dead Poets Society*. A year later they met up when Depardieu spent ten days with the Weirs at their Palm Beach house in Sydney.

Depardieu worked with Weir the way he'd done with Truffaut and Blier, jotting down ideas, telling his story and laughing about it all. They'd take plenty of breaks in the sea, 'long, slow swims like two old ladies', building up their friendship. They were birds of a feather. Depardieu admired Weir for making risky decisions and doing things 'slightly in excess'. In Weir, he had found another 'brother'. Weir, with his big nose, could easily be related to.

Depardieu met his co-star, Andie MacDowell, in New York when he flew over to present *Trop Belle Pour Toi* at the New York festival. Her film, *sex, lies and videotape*, had just been released and they clicked instantly. Depardieu says in the film's production notes that MacDowell was the type of woman he adores working with, 'a beautiful person with the laugh of a child'. It was clear that sparks would fly between them on screen. A year later, backed by Disney to the tune of $12 million, shooting began.

In *Green Card*, he plays an ungainly French composer who marries a vegetarian horticulturalist to obtain US citizenship – as represented by that coveted green card. She marries him in order to rent the perfect apartment in a marrieds-only block. They have to know everything about each other so as to convince the immigration people who are due to check up on them a few months later that the marriage is not one of convenience. A weekend together is arranged for them to get acquainted. The weekend is intolerable. It is spent arguing about everything from politics to how to make coffee. He finds her impossibly prissy. She thinks he's unspeakably boorish and calls him 'a silly French oaf'.

In the process of getting to know each other, little details of Depardieu's

Quiet times in Central Park with Andie MacDowell in Green Card, *1990*

real life are revealed through his character, Georges Fauré, such as having a father called René, and bearing tatoos on his arms which he obtained living with two prostitutes called Irène and Michèle. Other details, like his height (5′ 11″) and his weight ('*Ouf*, too much'!) also slip in.

MacDowell said she had been terrified of meeting Depardieu, not because 'he was a giant of the cinema but because I adored him! All my girlfriends are dying to meet him . . . He has such passion, he eats life . . . His greatest charm is that he makes you feel good about yourself.'

Green Card was the perfect bridgehead for the French actor to make his mark on the English-speaking movie market place. When he first received Weir's screenplay, he had it translated into French on cassette, but did not take Berlitz classes or hire a speaking coach. Instead, he explored his own difficulties with the language, turning them to an advantage. (On set, he and Weir communicated in both French – Weir is fluent – and English.) But as the big-money movie world talks in English, not French, Depardieu knew he had to get it right. His on-screen English had to be easily understandable for the mass audience. (His off-screen English sometimes isn't but it's always delivered with assurance as it careens vertiginously between the theatrical and the streetwise.) One reviewer wrote: 'Hearing English come from the familiar lips of France's leading acting export . . . is as jarring and intoxicating as finding your favourite doll come to life.'

For his English, Depardieu consulted Alfred Tomatis again, who gave him tapes of the sounds an Anglophone baby would hear in the womb. He learned his lines phonetically, not always knowing what they meant. Talking with him through an interpreter (he insists on having one present), it is evident that he is a good mimic and has a sharp ear. When he hears a new (English) word it rapidly becomes his own and he connects ideas very quickly.

'One day I must take two months off – or two years – and hit myself over the head with English until some of it sinks in,' he laughed at the *Green Card* press conference in Los Angeles. 'Not having English is like not playing the piano, which, as with my English, I do only on film. Perhaps I am desperate to learn but impossible to teach.'

Depardieu hit America dressed in character, in his trademark floppy brown knave-of-hearts haircut, *blouson*, jeans and black boots, enthusiastic demeanour in tact – but soon to be crushed. He arrived with Marie-France Vassel, the *Cyrano* makeup woman whom he brought over for the film, and virtually no entourage. His stay was for five months, a long haul away from home although he *did* shoot back on Concorde for the Tigné wine festival and spent seventy-four hours in Cannes when *Cyrano* played there to collect the Best Actor award. He was living in Manhattan's Surrey Hotel and was having trouble understanding the New York accents, difficulty finding good French food, even fresh chicken, and trying to cope with a surfeit of time alone 'to think too much'. He felt like an innocent tiptoeing through a deadly minefield. The Americans, he commented, had different ways of looking at things. 'New York is full of lost souls. It is a very violent city. It completely blew my mind. Even if I had dreamed it, it could never have come out this way. I could never live in America. It truly stupefied me. Too many things tie me to France – the wine, the directors, the food, my family . . .'

In an interview with *Vogue*'s Paul Chutkow, he tells a tale of how he got his knuckles rapped in New York over ladies' breasts.

'In France you can come right out and say: "You have superb breasts." Well, when I said in New York, "Oh, you have beautiful breasts", the women were completely shocked. And I would say, "No, no, I don't mean to be insulting or even suggestive; it's just because I find your breasts truly lovely. That is the right word, isn't it, *breasts?*" Which of course only got

Arriving at Le Bourget in his private plane with wife Elisabeth and daughter Julie after Cannes, 1990

me in deeper . . .' He doesn't like to provoke, though there's no doubting his fondness for getting reactions out of people – just his face provokes. Americans did, however, eventually accept him as he is, not as an actor, but as a Frenchman.

He also plunged into hot water when, at an event celebrating the splendour of Pommard, he sent a woman a card saying '*Après, bientôt*' ('Afterwards, soon') and received the card back with the impression of her husband's fist, smothered in burnt cork, returning the compliment, '*Après, bientôt* . . .' On 'Late Night with David Letterman', he perplexed his audience (and host) by telling them that he considered himself lucky as a kid, because 'my father was dead drunk all day'. His extended meditations on the nature of painting, philosophy and great literature went down particularly well. However, now that France has become the biggest European investor in US films, the Hollywood game is one an actor like Depardieu is going to have to play.

He has always been enamoured of the great American film comics: Charlie Chaplin, Buster Keaton, Harold Lloyd. In his opinion, comedy is the hardest form of acting to pull off. He is a massive fan of Orson Welles, who told him once when they lunched together that he never used his real nose in his films, preferring to use a fake, because his was too small. Depardieu has also been referred to as a French Woody Allen ('he has power and violence, I'm just violent with my little contradictions') and is constantly compared to Brando, De Niro, James Dean ('Why compare? We are all just trying to communicate').

Depardieu says in America he relates most to the films of Martin Scorsese and Francis Ford Coppola, as they, for him, 'translate best about minority groups and their tragedies'. He can't cope with the high-impact American blockbuster.

'Maybe I'm stupid, but I don't understand a lot of them. Maybe I'm too old. I prefer historical movies and classical drama, and I love sentimental stuff. No amount of money will get me doing rubbish in America. I'm no Schwarzenegger without the muscle. I don't want to make special-effects films. I am a special effect alone on my own,' he said at the end of *Green Card*, before flying out to start work in France two days later on Claude Berri's *Uranus*. By that time the deep grey eyes had the hint of a hunted man, the slave-in-chains look. He needed to return home.

Depardieu's passion for the films of Satyajit Ray, the Indian director of unchallenged perception, had been growing for some time. To Depardieu, Ray is a visionary and an *auteur*, one of the last of the great masters. Like Depardieu, he has made dozens of films, all of them based in the reality of his own society of Indian villages and city life. Depardieu recently went into partnership with France's leading producer (and, needless to say, friend), Daniel Toscan du Plantier, formerly of Gaumont, to co-produce Ray's next film, *The Branches of the Tree*, and the two of them commuted from Paris to Calcutta for the project.

'The life of a serious Bengali cineaste is a hard one,' says du Plantier, 'when faced with the huge commercial power of a popular production made in Hindi. Gérard can bring aid from France for this film and Ray's films to come.' Jack Lang (France's Minister of Culture) had also promised financial aid and Depardieu has set up a foundation to preserve the artistic legacy of Satyajit Ray, who has become – perhaps inevitably – a close friend.

For a man with worldwide interests, Depardieu appears to have remained an idealistic *homme d'affaires* (businessman), even though the battle of being tough versus being vulnerable is still being fought. 'I'm not happy in confrontations, whatever they may be.'

His major confrontation in 1990 was the on-going junket with the American and foreign press to promote *Green Card*. A press and TV campaign that Disney had pumped $5 million into ensured his first stab at US stardom would reap huge rewards. Holed up in Los Angeles's Ma Maison, he amused the troops with jokes of making the film on a holiday visa, *sans* green card, and said that if this film were a hamburger, it would be made with good beef and blue cheese, not beef-mix and ketchup. He was nervous but elated, sculpting his conversation with his mouth, eyes and hands.

He is one of the few actors who can handle unconventional sex on screen, and I asked him how he felt about conventional love scenes on screen. What about kissing?

'Ah, the kiss!' he exclaimed, lighting up another Gitane and stroking the little moustache he had grown for *Merci La Vie* (*Thank You Life*). 'I have done all the sex scenes you can imagine, but kissing on film is the most troublesome. Especially kissing a man. It is frightening, you are sweating, it is like a rape, very violent,' he said, using the inflammatory words '*viol*' and '*violence*.' 'The most frightening thing is while you know that the sex scenes are never true, because actual sex isn't possible on screen – I like sex too much to feel like acting at the same time – but with the kiss it *can* be true.'

He gave an enigmatic little chuckle and said that these days he was keen to make more love stories – *histoires d'amour* – but lamented that 'almost everybody won't consider me for those parts, because they think I am too big'. The man who made big bellies both sexy and fashionable caressed his. 'I have to admit I am pretty huge right now!' He gets a certain pleasure out of flouting the conventions of the new health-conscious movie hierarchy.

All morning Monsieur Depardieu was the perfect interviewee. He had been drinking the hotel's best wine since breakfast and was on form. But at lunchtime, abruptly, imperceptibly, his mood changed. He became maudlin and homesick, and threw a private screen around him to keep out the pressures. He cancelled the afternoon's interviews and retired to his room. As he said, 'fame brings too many assholes to beam at'. He'd done his day's beaming. Later I bumped into him striding along the passage. He greeted me cordially with a warm handshake and strode on, chased by unknown demons.

Hilary Clark, vice-president of international publicity for Disney's Buena Vista Pictures, recalls her days with him on the promotion campaign:

Depardieu beaming

'Beyond anything I had ever read about him or observed from his films, I was struck by his genuine naturalness and warmth. He was completely spontaneous. Everyone around him felt at ease. It was contagious.

'But then, each afternoon, he would get melancholy. From the things he said, we got the feeling that by the time he had spread his big heart around to everyone else, there was none left over for himself. I don't think he has any idea how lovable he is – but then again, that is the source of his charm.'

Even just shaking hands, he tries to pass you something of himself.

20

Prizes and Pillage

Four weeks after *Green Card*'s Christmas Day opening, Depardieu picked up a Golden Globe for Best Comic Actor. A couple of weeks later his Cyrano earned him a nomination from Hollywood's most exclusive club, the Oscars. A couple of weeks after that he won the Best Actor César, presented by Rosanna Arquette, who called him Gérard Dipardiou and blushed. His star was rising fast in the show-business heavens. A few weeks after that, he attended the Golden Globe Awards. For most of the Hollywood cast assembled for the 1991 ceremony at the Beverly Hilton Hotel, it was their first live glimpse of the French actor.

Sitting among Tinseltown luminaries like Bruce Willis and Demi Moore, Julia Roberts and Kiefer Sutherland, Jeremy Irons, Patrick Swayze, Warren Beatty and his sister Shirley Maclaine, he was sweating and awkward. He was having trouble coping with the genteel pecks that pass for kisses in Hollywood, and attempting not to crush X-ray thin women in $10,000 dresses when they offered a cheek or refined hand to him. As the temperature inside the room spiralled above the glitter of the perfect tans, toupées, halogen teeth and tightly-tucked faces, Depardieu mopped his brow, ripped off his bow-tie and undid the top buttons of his dress shirt. He says he felt like a spectator and had forgotten he was one of those nominated. They announced Julia Roberts's name for Best Actress. Next came his name: the award for Best Actor was his.

Almost perplexed, he clambered out of his chair and shambled towards the stage. An awed silence fell upon the Americans as they watched this study in extremes, the earthy and the cerebral, as he grappled for the right words, sweat pouring from his forehead.

A week later, at The Savoy for the London *Evening Standard* British Film Awards, he was given the biggest cheer of the night when Cherie Lunghi, the actress presenting the award, called him up on stage to make an unscheduled speech to an admiring audience. *Cyrano* had reached the coveted number one box-office position in London. As he left the stage, he bent to retrieve gallantly a guest's dinner napkin that had fallen at her feet.

Time magazine's 25.02.91 issue then ran a profile on Depardieu, headed *Cyrano Takes Hollywood* and asked if France's top movie actor could translate his 'primal energy into global stardom'? *Bien sûr!* said the writer, Richard Corliss, *Time*'s film critic. Corliss is a former editor of *Film Comment*, which, in its March/April 1978 issue, had carried a story *Depardieu: French Primitive* by Harry Stein. This four-page interview billed him as France's 'most important young actor'. In it Depardieu told many colourful tales of his life, especially his childhood, including one about a bus-stop incident concerning himself, aged nine, and his teenage buddy, Jacky Merveille.

This is Stein's story – denied by Depardieu – as it appeared: '. . . the girl, a brunette in her early twenties, was waiting for a bus when the teenager and the nine-year old began teasing her. "One thing led to another and, hup!!" – Depardieu suddenly rises halfway out of his chair, like an animal bounding after prey – "that was that." He pauses. "It was normal. After that I had plenty of rapes, too many to count."'

In *Time* almost thirteen years and forty films later, Corliss resuscitated the story: 'And what of his story that at nine he went along on his first rape? "Yes." And after that there were many rapes? "Yes," he says, with an astonishing frankness, "but it was absolutely normal in those circumstances. That all makes me laugh. That was part of my childhood," as growing up near a US base must, inevitably, have been.'

By March this quotation had sparked an outcry of fury from women across America. The *National Inquirer* carried the headline 'Oscar Nominee Admits He was a Rapist' and the *Washington Post* billed him similarly. America's National Organization for Women director, Tammy Bruce, said that the actor should make a public apology and pay money to women's rights movements. 'It is an outrage to honor him at the Academy Awards,' she cried. Depardieu unequivocally denied making the statements and said that it would be 'perhaps accurate to say that I had sexual experience at an early age . . . But rape, never. I respect women too much.' He had always been treated fairly by the American press, and was bewildered and deeply wounded by what had happened and by such accusations.

'I have a wife and children and do not intend to be treated as a rapist,' he added. *Time* refused the actor's demand that the passage be retracted. (It was reported that Depardieu's lawyers were to file an action but at the time of going to press in July 1991, *Time* informed me that no action had yet been filed.)

It appears that in the *Time* interview, which was conducted on tape in French, the word he used was '*assister*', translated as 'participated in'. Depardieu's camp contends that his words were translated incorrectly. The verb '*assister*' in French means 'to be present at', not 'to help' or 'to take part in'. (It may well be that Depardieu may have said '*vol*' meaning 'theft', not '*viol*' meaning 'rape'.) According to Jean-Paul Rappeneau, who was in Hollywood, French lawyers in New York had listened to the tape recorded by *Time* and had said it did not contain the accusations against Depardieu. While *Time* stood by its story, the French remembered that no actor unable to express himself in English, has yet won the Oscar. People even referred back to the 1950 José Ferrer/*Cyrano* Oscar ceremony, when the American press claimed that Ferrer was like others a crypto-Communist. *Le Monde* claimed that José Ferrer had been accused of rape during his adolescence, also on the eve of the Oscar ceremony. He got the Oscar. 'I am starting to believe that Cyrano invites destruction,' Rappeneau said.

The French were devastated by the attack. Depardieu's press attaché in Paris, Claude Davy, said that 'when he said he took part in his first rape at nine, it was just a joke to show that he was a man before his time'. Jacques Attali, aide to President Mitterrand, said: 'It is vile defamation with high financial yield, since the stakes in the coming days are considerable . . . with all the fall-out tied to the Oscars'. Jack Lang, Minister of Culture, said he was outraged by a 'violent, mean and lowly' press attack against Depardieu. Marguerite Duras, asked about Depardieu's remarks, said dismissively, 'When I was eight and a half I stole an apple from the garden.'

Dr Pilorgé, father of Michel and honorary president of the National Association for Rural Medicine, posed the question of the physical side of the matter: 'To be a rapist at nine is simply impossible,' he said. The British tabloids, meanwhile, leapt in to make mincemeat of Depardieu with the fervour of Waterloo revisited.

Hollywood and hypocrisy have always gone together, but seldom so blatantly. It is an industry known for its prudishness over things like sex and nudity. More than twenty years ago, there was controversy when Yves Montand, already unpopular in Hollywood for supporting Communist causes, admitted that he had slept with Marilyn Monroe during the filming of *Let's Make Love*. Other tales along these lines include Polish-born, French-nationalised director Roman Polanski having to flee America for the safety of Paris after he was indicted on a charge of sexual intercourse with a thirteen-year-old girl (France does not permit its nationals to be extradited on sex charges); Jean Seberg was boycotted because she slept with a Black Panther; and Ingrid Bergman was denounced as 'Hollywood's apostle of degradation' after having a son out of wedlock with Roberto Rossellini. Perhaps Montand's warning to his fellow countrymen to beware of American puritanism and understand that they 'are like that . . . touchy about things that seem a joke to us' hit the right nerve.

Depardieu did not attend the Oscar ceremony at the Dorothy Chandler Pavilion in Los Angeles on 25 March 1991. With the 4,000-member-plus Los Angeles chapter of the National Organization for Women massing their troops for the awards it is hardly surprising. Instead he made an appearance on Europe One television from the Indian Ocean island of Mauritius where he was shooting *Mon Père, Ce Héros*, voicing his anger and hurt at having been defamed. Miles from home, he remained there, at a loss to know whether the affair would blow over or permanently tarnish his image with English-speaking audiences.

In the event, an obscure film about Turkish immigrants to Switzerland, *Journey of Hope*, directed by Xavier Koller, won the Best Foreign Film award, and Jeremy Irons got the golden statue for Best Actor for his portrayal of Claus von Bulow in Barbet Schroeder's fictionalised version of the Sunny von Bulow case, *Reversal of Fortune*.

Depardieu once said in an interview: 'The Oscars are the great feast of cinema but I think it's better to be nominated than to win. Not many actors survive the winning with their normality.' He found out that nominees can also take the rap.

L'Affaire Depardieu came at a bad time for him. In spite of suddenly being flavour of the month with the Anglo-Saxon nations, underneath there had been rumblings for some time of a real mid-life crisis. Although in a position to fly in a private plane and have whatever he wanted materially, he was apparently in analysis again and definitely not *bien dans sa peau*. 'I am miserable in spite of everything,' he agonised. The mercurial freestyle had been replaced by melancholic ramblings. Ageing had made him scared of losing his panache.

'I'm at a delicate age,' he said in Los Angeles, rolling his eyes. 'I'm volatile, as they say of wine when it's in danger of turning into vinegar. I have the temperament of a wild man; I'm capable of doing anything. But it's not out of anger towards others. It's an anger towards myself. A total dejection which brings on masochism: I'm never in agreement with myself.'

He says it still with his whirlwind inventiveness but there is an overriding sense of profound insecurity. Life, he says, can be a nightmare, his biggest battle being with 'my excessiveness'.

'Middle age is tragic. If you're in your forties and you're the slightest bit of an artist or a creator, you have to keep moving.'

For Depardieu, ducking and diving to avoid a past that will not go away is a way of life. As he keeps saying, a zebra doesn't change its stripes. Diluting the past for various reasons is a way of life for many people, and for some French people *d'un âge certain*, the word 'collaboration' is still a dirty one even today, decades after the Second World War finished.

Straight after *Green Card*, Depardieu sped home to work on *Uranus*, Claude Berri's £9 million adaptation of Marcel Aymé's polemical novel which challenged the enduring myth that most French were solidly united in resistance to the German occupation and the Vichy régime's collaboration with the Nazis. One of the toughest pictures to be made in France about that period, reactions were mixed when it came out. French Communists fumed about the 'unworthy' depiction of their resistance heroes and skeletons twitched in many cupboards around France.

It is by far Depardieu's most political film, and he plays Léopold, a village café owner, drunk and poet caught in the twilight zone of 1945, between the old order and the new. Like the man himself, he is the poet who cannot escape the politics. Friends Michel Blanc and Philippe Noiret play a hen-pecked Communist and a schoolteacher and Depardieu's brother-in-law Patrick Bordier was production director. D.D. Productions had a slice of the action and, of course, working with Berri, directing his first film since *Manon des Sources*, meant being well and truly back with 'family'.

Depardieu joked about how Léopold the bartender was such an easy role for him to play, downing bottles of wine without a pause, causing havoc in a prison cell and passionately reciting *Andromaque*, wondering what Racine drank while he worked. Depardieu loved making it. He said Léopold had given him his best ever death scene, 'the sort actors would die for'. Léopold's death, a huge man falling in his bar among the tables and chairs, is one Depardieu carries out with visceral realism and weightless clumsiness.

'It's funny, in all of my films where I was hanging or burned or died in very violent ways, I would think about actually going through all of these deaths. When you imagine a death you really live it. You make your peace. Death is the ultimate retirement. I don't have a suicidal nature. For me it would be a heart attack. I don't want to suffer, like Steve McQueen [who died of lung cancer in 1980]. I don't want to make my family suffer.'

Uranus came as part of what could be considered a dream year for an actor – *Cyrano*, then *Green Card* and *Uranus*, all followed by a sizeable clutch of awards. But Depardieu, whose ups and downs have levelled out his life from the start, was cautious. He could never have anticipated the rape scandal and, when it came, it left him reeling. But he knew he would be up again as quickly as he had plummeted downwards.

'In America, when they like you it's okay, when they don't like you it's still okay because they tell you, but they won't lend you a *velo* to go to the airport and get out,' he joked. In a huge interview in *Paris-Match* he said: 'I have been dirtied but I want to make myself clean very quickly.'

As wartime barkeeper Léopold in Uranus, *1991*

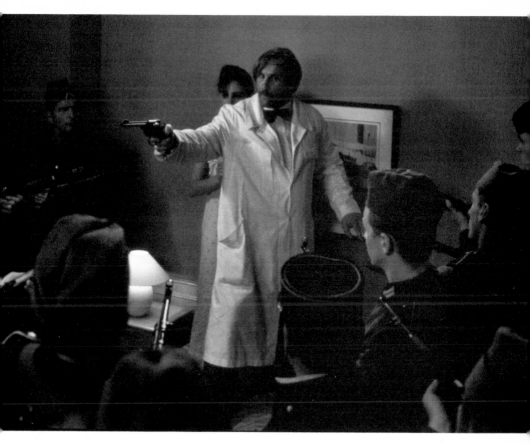

Depardieu as Dr Marc Antoine in Merci La Vie, *1991*

Hardly had the dust in the rape scandal settled than fierce demonstrations broke out over his next film *Merci La Vie* which delighted him. Before it was released, he jovially described the film as being about 'AIDS and Nazis, a punch in the stomach of society'. It was his sixth with Blier and made with his 'family' of Jean Carmet, Michel Blanc, Jean-Louis Trintignant and Serge Gainsbourg's daughter Charlotte. In it he plays a louche doctor who specialises in treating patients suffering from the AIDS virus and encourages a young woman with AIDS (played by Anouk Grinberg) to sleep with men so he can profit from their plight.

It is a raw and renegade film, even for Blier, and infuriated members of the public attacked him in the street and threatened to do the same to Depardieu. AIDS sufferers felt exploited, women felt relegated to the sex-object category and the medical profession was upset at the suggestion that some may be cashing in on the virus. From his retreat in the Indian Ocean, Depardieu merely laughed at having once again successfully overstepped the *bourgeois* tidemark. *Merci La Vie* became a box-office hit and there is talk of a Hollywood studio acquiring the rights to remake it in English. It was again a case of Life imitating Art imitating Life imitating . . .

'My life is a screen. My "normal" life has become completely abstract. I am a bit like Tom Baxter, the hero of Woody Allen's *The Purple Rose of Cairo*, who steps off the silver screen to live a romance instead of, like everybody else, escaping into one.

'The important thing about acting for me is communication. To open things inside of you that you don't really know yourself. If you look for them, you never find them. Picasso said, "I never look at anything. I find." I also find: a certain peace, the peace that comes when you accept the idea of what gives you pleasure.

'I have my life's programme, filled for two years in advance, with all kinds of wonderful stories. I have my escaping into reality. If my screen life all ended tomorrow, I'd do something else. I'd write, I'd make wine. I have other interests – I wouldn't die.'

There's always a job waiting for him at La Garoupe or Le Plage des Sports.

Epilogue

Pirandello once said that every actor is looking for a role for his house to feel like a home. Depardieu has found many homes already but still has a list of roles awaiting him that could create a large housing estate. In the smoky home of our hero-sized star, the unlikely sex symbol, box-office draw, Oscar nominee, and *voyou* that got away, the roles coil around one another tightly, leaving not a breath of air to spare.

There have been projects that never came off, like a Michelangelo Antonioni film in 1983 called *The Crew* that would have been made in America in English with Robert Duvall, and the new Kirk Douglas adventure, *Welcome to Veraz*, which Richard Bohringer got. There have also been his own projects which he has been talking about for years but has not yet found the wherewithal to do: a film about Vercingétorix, the Gallic liberator who pitted himself against the Roman occupation and was executed by Julius Cæsar, or a film on the Battle of Bouvines in which Philippe Auguste, King of France, fights the Comte de Boulogne with 3,000 cavalry galloping across the plains; or the Count of Monte Cristo or a film in Latin.

'I love history, because I didn't learn it at school. It's better to learn when you live the life of history . . .'

Perhaps the historical figure he cites the most in interviews is Gilles de Rais, a warrior of Joan of Arc's who helped Charles VII defeat the English, but was also a monster who organised bloodthirsty orgies and sacrificed children in his château.

185

'It's a very strong text and he is a huge character, but I am a bit frightened of playing Gilles de Rais on stage alone every night with the problem of knowing that he killed 240 children. It might be too hard ... I'm a little bit fragile now. I am pondering the life of Guillaume Apollinaire to add to my historical roles.' Depardieu visited the grave of the half-Italian, half-Polish poet (1880–1918) in Père Lachaise long before he had any roles.

For ages he has been mentioning how he and Dustin Hoffman are going to do something together, and more recently he was very taken with a scenario sent him by the New Zealand director, Jane Campion, auteur of *Sweetie* and *An Angel at My Table*. British director Alan Parker has said he would like to work with him and he heads Blake Edwards's list for Inspector Clouseau in MGM-Pathé's new Pink Panther film.

The Americans have already asked if he will do for them in English the film he was making at Oscar-time on the tropical island of Mauritius, *Mon Père, Ce Héros*. Produced by Jean-Louis Livi and D.D. Productions, it is directed by Gérard Lauzier, one of France's top cartoonists, and is a slice-of-life comedy about a chap and his daughter (Marie Gillian). The title comes from a quote in Victor Hugo's epic poem 'La Légende des Siècles' ('The Legend of the Centuries'): '*Mon père, ce héros, au sourire si doux*': 'My father, this hero with a gentle smile'.

Immediately afterwards, he and Livi returned to Paris to start work on *Tous les Matins du Monde* (*All the Mornings in the World*) with Daniel Auteuil and Anne Brochet co-starring, and Alain Corneau directing. Based on the life of seventeenth-century French composer and viola-player Marin Marais, an important musician who had nineteen children and performed at the court of Louis XIV, Depardieu's son Guillaume plays Marais as a young man while his father is Marais Elder. Depardieu says: 'Guillaume is more handsome than I am and much more sensible.' It is already known in the market place as *Amadeus Two*, as the story includes two rival musicians.

Somewhere between all that he appeared in a short film, with Michel Piccoli, Robin Williams and Jeremy Irons, directed by John Badman, for Discoveryland at the new Disney MGM Studios theme park outside Paris. During the summer of 1991, the 17th Moscow Film Festival paid special homage to Depardieu and London's Barbican Centre hosted a tribute to him with a season of twenty-four films in *Depardieu – Gérard Le Grand*. Readers of *The Observer* 'quite rightly repaired an omission by the Oscar voters' and selected him as Best Actor of the year.

With Livi, he will round off their trilogy together with *Colonel Chabert*, from Balzac's novel about a colonel who is buried during one of the wars of Napoleon and manages to dig his way out, only to be taken for mad. He returns to France to find his wife has remarried, his money has gone and himself believed dead. For Depardieu, it is a perfect vehicle. It has a touch of *Martin Guerre* about it and plenty of what he might have been had he not opted for acting. Chabert, in his old age, becomes a homeless, nameless vagabond. With Kenneth Branagh, meanwhile, he intends to make films of *Macbeth* and *Othello*, plays he and Elisabeth were planning to do on stage in Paris some time ago. 'Hamlet bores the shit out of me,' reveals Depardieu. 'He's such a little intellectual. Give me Othello, or Macbeth any day – at least he's got a real problem with God.'

But the film that will make or break the international market for Depardieu is, indubitably, *Christopher Columbus*, the story of the Genoese explorer who stumbled on America in 1492 thinking he had found a Western route to India. It's a multi-million pound English-language epic directed by Ridley Scott, and Depardieu describes Columbus as 'an Italian gypsy, who is also Jewish, who made journeys comparable to our conquering of space. He's often thought of as just a famous sailor but there's more to him than that. He took enormous risks, telling people the earth was round and keeping the Church happy by bringing in gold. He was driven by the gods and had a sacred faith, and then,' he adds slyly, 'you have the love story with Queen Isabella.' Love story? 'But, of course. If there was no love story, she wouldn't have given him seventeen boats.'

Depardieu is at it again, stirring, savouring, scouring the pot.

Awards

1973   Prix Gérard Philipe
1981   César: Best Actor – *Le Dernier Métro*
1982   Montreal Film Festival Best Actor – *Danton*
1983   Prix de l'Association des Cadres de l'Industrie Cinématographique
1984   US National Society of Film Critics: Best Actor – *Danton* and *Le Retour de Martin Guerre*
1985   Venice Film Festival: Best Actor – *Police*
1989   Fellowship of the British Film Institute
1990   Cannes Film Festival: Best Actor – *Cyrano de Bergerac*
1990   César: Best Actor of the Decade
1991   César: Best Actor – *Cyrano de Bergerac*
1991   Golden Globe: Best Actor – *Green Card*
1991   *The Observer*: Best Actor – *Cyrano de Bergerac*
1991   Moscow Film Festival: Special Prize

Filmography

1971:	*Le Cri du Cormoran le Soir Au-Dessus des Jonques*	Michel Audiard
	Un Peu de Soleil dans l'Eau Froide	Jacques Deray
1972:	*Le Viager*	Pierre Tchernia
	Le Tueur	Denys de la Patellière
	La Scoumoune	José Giovanni
1973:	*Au Rendezvous de la Mort Joyeuse*	Juan Buñuel
	L'Affaire Dominici	Claude Bernard-Aubert
	Nathalie Granger	Marguerite Duras
	Deux Hommes dans la Ville	José Giovanni
	Rude Journée pour la Reine	René Allio
1974:	*Les Gaspards*	Pierre Tchernia
	Les Valseuses	Bertrand Blier
	La Femme du Gange	Marguerite Duras
	Stavisky	Alain Resnais
	Vincent, François, Paul et les Autres	Claude Sautet
1975:	*Pas Si Méchant Que Ça*	Claude Goretta
	Sept Morts sur Ordonnance	Jacques Rouffio
1976:	*Maîtresse*	Barbet Schroeder
	Je t'Aime, Moi Non Plus	Serge Gainsbourg
	La Dernière Femme	Marco Ferreri
	1900	Bernardo Bertolucci
	Barocco	André Téchiné

1977:	René La Canne	Francis Girod
	Le Camion	Marguerite Duras
	Baxter, Vera Baxter	Marguerite Duras
	Dîtes-Lui que Je l'Aime	Claude Miller
	La Nuit tous les Chats sont Gris	Gérard Zingg
1978:	Préparez Vos Mouchoirs	Bertrand Blier
	Violanta	Daniel Schmid
	Rêve de Singe	Marco Ferreri
	La Femme Gauchère	Peter Handke
	Le Sucre	Jacques Rouffio
1979:	Les Chiens	Alain Jessua
	Le Grand Embouteillage	Luigi Comencini
	Buffet Froid	Bertrand Blier
1980:	Mon Oncle d'Amérique	Alain Resnais
	Rosy La Bourrasque	Mario Monicelli
	Le Dernier Métro	François Truffaut
	Loulou	Maurice Pialat
	Inspecteur La Bavure	Claude Zidi
	Je Vous Aime	Claude Berri
	Le Choix des Armes	Alain Corneau
1981:	La Femme d'à Côté	François Truffaut
	La Chèvre	Francis Veber
1982:	Le Retour de Martin Guerre	Daniel Vigne
	Le Grand Frère	Francis Girod
1983:	Danton	Andrzej Wajda
	La Lune dans le Caniveau	Jean-Jacques Beineix
	Les Compères	Francis Veber
1984:	Fort Saganne	Alain Corneau
	Le Tartuffe	Gérard Depardieu
	Rive Droite, Rive Gauche	Philippe Labro
1985:	Police	Maurice Pialat
	Une Femme ou Deux	Daniel Vigne
1986:	Tenue de Soirée	Bertrand Blier
	Jean de Florette	Claude Berri
	Je Hais les Acteurs	Gérard Krawczyk
	Rue du Départ	Tony Gatlif
	Les Fugitifs	Francis Veber
1987:	Sous le Soleil de Satan	Maurice Pialat

1988:	*Drôle d'Endroit*	François Dupeyron
	Camille Claudel	Bruno Nuytten
1989:	*Deux*	Claude Zidi
	Trop Belle Pour Toi	Bertrand Blier
	I Want to go Home	Alain Resnais
1990:	*Cyrano de Bergerac*	Jean-Paul Rappeneau
1991:	*Green Card*	Peter Weir
	Uranus	Claude Berri
	Merci La Vie	Bertrand Blier
	Mon Père, Ce Héros	Gérard Lauzier
	Tous les Matins du Monde	Alain Corneau
	Christopher Columbus	Ridley Scott

Acknowledgements

My thanks go to all the people who took the time and energy to contribute to this book. I am grateful more than any words can express to Judy Olivier, Michael Popham and my father Ginger for their hours of reading; Tony Crawley for sharing his early Depardieu material with me; James Woodall for the editing; Pearson Phillips for the anecdotes; Marie-Pierre Moine and Françoise Lina-Flowers for their translating; Stephen Gray for the moral support; Derek Elley, Robert Rider, Claire Engel and Jean-Luc Nivaggioni for helping with the films and videos.

Some of the factual and quoted matter in this book is based on previously published material. The list of publications that follows records my grateful thanks: *Time, The New York Times, The Face, Lears, Time Out, American Film Monthly, Studio, Première, Newsweek, The Independent, Washington Post, Newsday, Fame, Daily Mail, The Observer, Paris-Match, The Guardian, Interview, The Sunday Times.*

The following illustrations appear by kind permission of:
The BFI (49, 120), The Tony Crawley Collection (33, 42, 53, 59, 88, 111, 117, 135, 138, 140, 183), Gamma (97), Ronald Grant (82, 137, 150, 151, 161), Frank Spooner (108, 125, 126, 132, 139, 144, 155), Steven Walgren (175), Channel 4 (74, 86, 95), Maurice Croze (10, 12), Marianne Gray (8, 15, 30, 52, 103, 145, 154, 163, 170, 182), The John Kobal Collection (40, 44, 48, 62, 64, 69, 72, 78, 79, 113, 127, 128), Retna (157), Sygma (38, 98, 122, 165, 166, 172).

Bibliography

Gérard Depardieu – l'autodidacte inspiré – Robert Chazal (Hatier 1982)
Gérard Depardieu – Christian Gonzalez (Edilig 1985)
Gérard Depardieu – Olivier Dazat (Seghers 1988)
Gérard Depardieu – Georges Cohen (Editions J'ai Lu 1988)
Lettres Volées – Gérard Depardieu (J-C Lattès 1988)